EFFECTIVE LEADERSHIP SKILLS FOR MANAGERS

EIGHT KEY SKILLS FOR CAREER ADVANCEMENT, CONFLICT RESOLUTION, AND CULTIVATING EXCEPTIONAL TEAMS

ELSE PUBLICATIONS

CONTENTS

INTRODUCTION

Imagine you are at the forefront of a high-stakes project. The clock is ticking, the pressure mounts, and out of the blue, your team hits a snag —a conflict brings everything to a screeching halt. Here, in this whirlwind of challenges, lies the true test of leadership.

But what if you had a toolkit at your disposal, one that could turn confusion into harmony and chaos into productivity? That's precisely what this book offers: a treasure trove of strategies for the modern leader, designed to navigate the most turbulent of waters with grace and effectiveness.

Indeed, navigating the complexities of management is no small feat. Your decision to explore this book likely sprang from facing real-world challenges in your role as a leader or manager. It's not just about resolving conflicts, bridging communication gaps, or keeping your team motivated. These are significant issues, but they are often just the tip of the iceberg.

As you turn the pages of this book, you might see reflections on your own journey in management. Perhaps it's the challenge of aligning a diverse team toward a common goal, or the continuous quest to balance innovation with operational efficiency. Maybe it's the subtle nuances of fostering a culture of inclusivity and respect in an ever-diverse workplace. Or, it could be the personal aspiration to grow as a leader, refine your approach, and expand your influence.

This book is an acknowledgment of these unspoken challenges and aspirations. It is crafted not just as a guide, but as a mirror reflecting the complex, sometimes turbulent world of modern leadership. The insights and strategies within these pages are responses to the silent questions that often linger in the minds of managers and leaders in various sectors.

The importance of leadership skills in today's world stretches far beyond the traditional office environment. As the business landscape evolves, diversity in leadership has emerged as a key element for organizational success. This shift toward diverse leadership is rooted in the recognition of its numerous benefits.

Leaders from varied backgrounds bring a spectrum of perspectives, enriching the decision-making process with their diverse experiences and insights. This diversity is a catalyst for innovative thinking and creative problem-solving, essential in a competitive global market. Moreover, when leadership reflects the diversity of its workforce, it creates a more engaging and inclusive environment. Employees often feel more connected and valued in such settings, leading to higher motivation and job satisfaction.

Crucially, diverse leadership isn't just a matter of social responsibility or ethical management. It's a strategic advantage. Studies consistently show that companies with diverse leadership teams tend to be more innovative and financially successful. For example, According to a McKinsey report, companies that have ethnically diverse executive teams are statistically 36% more likely to achieve higher profitability compared to their counterparts (*Diverse Businesses Outperform Their Peers*, 2021). This advantage stems from the ability of diverse leadership to tap into a wider array of markets and customer needs, fostering better business strategies and outcomes.

The journey into leadership is a personal one, and this book aims to be a companion along that path. It offers not just solutions, but perspectives—not just strategies, but reflections. It invites you to delve deeper into your leadership style and explore new ways of thinking and acting that resonate with the unique demands of your role.

Building on this foundation, this book emerges as a manual and a practical guide replete with actionable strategies. It's about putting theory into action, offering you the tools to adeptly handle conflicts, communicate with clarity, and inspire your team. These insights serve as immediate instruments for transformation, allowing you to apply what you learn directly to your day-to-day leadership challenges. Consider this book as an investment in your professional journey, providing you with the knowledge to make informed decisions, cultivate a dynamic work environment, and chart a path to a prosperous career. The strategies and insights contained herein are designed to be both accessible and impactful, ensuring you can apply them effectively in your role as a leader.

At the heart of this book is the LEAD STAR framework, a nuanced approach tailored for the modern leader. Covering eight essential areas, this framework is a balanced amalgamation of actionable strategies, emotional intelligence, and personal development, each designed to address specific leadership challenges comprehensively. This comprehensive model is your roadmap to mastering eight essential leadership skills:

1. **Listen and communicate:** Sharpen your ability to engage in meaningful dialogue.
2. **Empower teams:** Cultivate a spirit of collaboration and unity.
3. **Analyze and decide:** Hone your strategic thinking and decision-making prowess.
4. **Develop relationships:** Build networks of trust and cooperation.

5. **Stimulate motivation:** Inspire and drive your team toward excellence.
6. **Tackle conflicts:** Navigate disputes with agility and understanding.
7. **Awareness of emotions:** Develop emotional intelligence for deeper connections.
8. **Regulate time and tasks:** Master the art of delegation and time management.

Embracing the LEAD STAR framework, you can expect a holistic enhancement in your leadership skills. This approach includes a deeper understanding of team dynamics, enriched communication skills, refined decision-making abilities, and stronger relationship-building techniques. These improvements lead to more cohesive teams, effective conflict resolution, and a noticeable boost in productivity and morale. This framework prepares you to navigate the complexities of leadership, setting the stage for your advancement and evolution as an empathetic and impactful leader.

Leaders across various industries have applied these strategies to great effect and they have attributed their leadership success to the principles outlined in the LEAD STAR framework. Their stories are testaments to the transformative power of these methods. We will talk more about this method as we go along.

This book is your gateway to a leadership style that's both fulfilling and effective. Envision a future where you steer through challenges with confidence and where your team is not just performing but excelling. That's the journey you're about to embark on.

The path to exceptional leadership is often laden with obstacles, and this book is a compilation of valuable lessons and insights gathered from both in-depth research and real-world experiences. It's a guide designed to arm you with the knowledge and tools essential for excelling in your role as a leader.

CHAPTER 1
LISTEN AND COMMUNICATE: EFFECTIVE DIALOGUE ESSENTIALS

"The art of effective listening is essential to clear communication and clear communication is necessary for management success."

JAMES CASH PENNEY

D id you know that a staggering 70% of business mistakes are due to poor communication? This research underlines the critical importance of effective communication in the workplace, highlighting that between 70% to 80% of corporate business intelligence projects fail due to poor communication between IT and business (*Does Effective Communication Matter in the Workplace*, 2023).

Effective communication is not just a valuable skill; it is a significant contributor to business success and personal career growth. For instance, it enhances team building, as teams that communicate effectively create a more enjoyable workplace and are more enthused to collaborate. Moreover, it plays a pivotal role in boosting business growth, fostering innovation, improving productivity, and increasing efficiency. Clear communication helps managers understand their employees' talents and assign tasks more effectively, leading to a smoother workflow and reduced instances of miscommunication.

By the end of this chapter, you will have gained insights into the importance of clear messaging in leadership and acquired practical techniques for impactful communication. These skills are crucial for your role as a manager, enhancing your ability to convey ideas, listen actively, and engage in meaningful dialogues that inspire and motivate your teams. Let's embark on this journey to elevate your communication prowess and become a leader who inspires action and drives progress.

THE ART OF EFFECTIVE COMMUNICATION

At the heart of every great leader's communication strategy lies a clear and compelling core message. This message encapsulates the leader's vision, values, and goals. It's the North Star that guides both the leader and their team.

The essential role of communication in leadership encompasses several key aspects:

- **Alignment with organizational goals:** Leaders' effective communication ensures employees understand and align with organizational and individual goals, leading to better results, increased job satisfaction, and higher morale.
- **Inspiration and motivation:** Effective communication is crucial for leaders to clearly define objectives and expectations, boosting team efficiency, engagement, and performance. Alternatively, poor communication can diminish motivation and productivity.
- **Awareness of challenges and opportunities:** Strong leadership communication keeps team members informed about the organization's challenges and opportunities, enabling informed decision-making that benefits the company's overall performance.

Enhancing communication in leadership involves several strategies, such as the following examples:

- **Be authentic:** Embrace your unique personality and life experiences. Authenticity in leadership fosters trust and builds genuine connections with your team.
- **Be visible:** Openness, such as an open-door policy, signals accessibility and a willingness to engage, making you more approachable.
- **Listen:** Active listening, including observing non-verbal cues, is essential. It shows respect and helps in understanding and addressing team concerns effectively.
- **Communicate often:** Regular communication keeps the team aligned and involved. Sharing updates and ideas regularly helps maintain team cohesion and engagement.

- **Encourage input:** Actively seek your team's feedback. Their insights can be instrumental in making informed decisions and driving improvements.
- **Share stories:** Sharing your personal experiences, especially when giving feedback, makes you more relatable and helps in delivering constructive criticism.
- **Walk the walk:** Consistency in what you say and do enhances your credibility. It's important to model the behavior you expect from your team.
- **Adapt your leadership style:** Understand that each team member is unique. Customizing your communication style to fit individual preferences can be more impactful.
- **Be transparent:** Keeping the team informed about organizational goals and challenges promotes a culture of openness and shared responsibility.
- **Ask open-ended questions:** Encouraging team members to elaborate on their thoughts fosters deeper understanding and engagement.

COMMON COMMUNICATION PITFALLS IN MANAGEMENT

Effective management hinges significantly on proficient communication. However, common pitfalls often hinder this process, leading to misunderstandings, reduced morale, and inefficiency. From failing to clearly articulate a vision to not adequately considering the audience, these communication errors can significantly impact leadership effectiveness and team dynamics.

- **Avoiding or procrastinating:** Leaders who delay crucial conversations often create an environment where problems fester and grow, leading to increased workplace tensions and unresolved issues.
- **Confusing facts and opinions:** When leaders mix personal opinions with facts, it leads to confusion and mistrust among team members, undermining the reliability of the information shared.
- **Rushing:** Communicating in haste often results in half-baked messages that are prone to misinterpretation, leading to errors and misunderstandings.
- **Sugarcoating:** Leaders who avoid conveying hard truths risk creating a culture lacking transparency and trust, as employees may feel they are not getting the whole picture.
- **Delivering feedback too aggressively:** Aggressive feedback can harm employee morale and performance, as it can come across as intimidating or demoralizing rather than constructive.
- **Using a feedback sandwich:** This method, where criticism is sandwiched between compliments, can dilute the impact of the critique and confuse the recipient about the main message.
- **Choosing the wrong communication channels:** Using inappropriate channels for communication can lead to distortions in the message and reduce its overall effectiveness.
- **Letting yourself get hijacked by your emotions:** Emotional responses in professional communication can cloud judgment, reduce objectivity, and lead to decisions or

statements that may not be in the best interest of the team or project.

Common pitfalls often derail this process, leading to miscommunications and a lack of alignment within teams. These pitfalls include the following 10 mistakes:

- **Mistake #1: Your vision lacks clarity:** A leader's vision serves as a guiding star. When it's not clear, it can create confusion, making it challenging for the team to follow and align with the objectives effectively.
- **Mistake #2: You haven't analyzed your audience:** Understanding who you're communicating with is key. It's about knowing their expectations, experiences, and how they process information, which ensures your message is received and understood as intended.
- **Mistake #3: You're using only one communication channel:** Diverse messages require diverse channels. Limiting yourself to one medium can restrict the reach and impact of your communication, possibly leaving some team members out of the loop.
- **Mistake #4: You haven't asked for feedback:** Feedback is a valuable tool for growth. It provides insight into how your communication is perceived and offers opportunities for improvement and adjustment.
- **Mistake #5: You've failed to explain the context:** Context is the backbone of effective communication. Without it, messages can be misinterpreted, losing their relevance and significance.
- **Mistake #6: You haven't reinforced your message:** Repetition is a powerful tool in communication. It ensures that key points are understood and remembered, reinforcing the message's importance and ensuring alignment.
- **Mistake #7: You haven't visualized your vision:** Visualization brings abstract concepts to life. It makes your

vision more tangible and relatable, helping your team grasp and connect with it more deeply.

- **Mistake #8: You've focused on "what" and "how" but not "why":** Explaining the "why" adds depth to your communication. It gives your team a reason to care and be invested in the vision and goals.
- **Mistake #9: Your vision is too ambitious or not ambitious enough:** The right level of ambition in your vision is crucial. It should be challenging yet attainable, inspiring yet realistic.
- **Mistake #10: You haven't conveyed your determination:** Your determination is infectious. Showing your commitment and passion can motivate and inspire your team to adopt the same level of dedication.

Real-Life Examples of Communication

Here are some real-life examples of communication breakdown in the workplace:

- When instructions are vague or incomplete, employees often make errors or delay tasks, leading to project inefficiencies and potential financial losses.
- Body language plays a crucial role in communication. Misreading these cues can lead to misunderstandings within teams, affecting morale and cooperation.
- Diverse workplaces can face communication challenges due to different native languages, resulting in confusion and hampering effective collaboration.
- Without regular and constructive feedback, employees can become disengaged, leading to job dissatisfaction and lower productivity.
- Emotional miscommunication can cause stress, misunderstandings, and reduced workplace productivity, impacting overall business performance.

- Bombarding employees with too much information can overwhelm them, leading to mistakes and inefficiency in task execution.
- Inadequate communication with clients can result in unmet expectations and strained relationships, potentially leading to lost business opportunities.

TECHNIQUES FOR CLEAR AND IMPACTFUL MESSAGING

Now, there are certain techniques that, when implemented, can significantly enhance workplace communication, fostering a more efficient, engaged, and harmonious working environment. Let's have a look at some of them.

- **Slow it down:** Taking the time to articulate thoughts clearly is vital. It involves speaking at a pace that allows listeners to process the information and provides them with the opportunity to grasp complex ideas more effectively.

- **Stop the slang, dawg:** Use standard language for clarity and to ensure everyone, regardless of background, understands your message.
- **Be an active listener:** Engage fully with the speaker by making sure you fully understand their words and non-verbal cues and respond thoughtfully.
- **Ask questions in several ways:** Sometimes, what seems clear to one person might be ambiguous to another. Ask questions or restate points differently to ensure clear understanding and avoid ambiguities.
- **Don't fill the void:** Embracing silence in conversations allows for thoughtful responses and the processing of information. So, allow pauses in conversation.
- **Know your audience:** Adapt your communication style to match the audience's knowledge and preferences for more effective communication.
- **Clarity is key:** Clear communication is about being straightforward and avoiding unnecessary complexity. It involves structuring your message in a logical, easy-to-follow manner, using simple language and avoiding ambiguity.
- **Being attentive:** Process and understand the message, responding in a way that acknowledges the speaker's perspective.
- **Choose the right medium:** Select the most effective medium (email, call, meeting) for your message to enhance clarity and reception.
- **Non-verbal communication:** Be aware of and use facial expressions, gestures, and tone to complement and enhance your verbal message.
- **Practice empathy:** Empathy in communication is to understand others' feelings and viewpoints to build stronger, more respectful workplace relationships.
- **Be concise:** Keep communication concise and focused on the key message for better attention and understanding.

- **Feedback and follow-up:** Encourage feedback for open dialogue and follow-up to confirm understanding and action steps.

Tips on Adapting Communication Styles to Different Audiences

Effective communication hinges on the ability to adapt your messaging to suit your audience. Utilizing various techniques to achieve this can significantly enhance engagement with your audience, leading to efficient and successful interactions.

- **Understand who your audience is and what motivates people:** Deeply understand your audience's cultural, professional, and personal backgrounds to effectively tailor your message, aligning with their values, goals, and interests.
- **Communicate your point clearly and through various mediums:** Use various platforms and mediums, like visual aids or digital media, to reinforce your message consistently and understandably across all channels.
- **Check your bias:** Every communicator brings their own set of biases to the table, whether they're aware of them or not. Regularly reflect on and check personal biases to ensure your communication is fair, respectful, and inclusive.
- **Open up and be vulnerable:** Vulnerability in communication can break down barriers and forge deeper connections. Sharing personal experiences and challenges can humanize you and create a trusting, relatable environment.
- **Identify your audience:** Identifying your audience goes beyond surface-level attributes like age or job title. Go beyond basic demographics to grasp your audience's mindset and preferences, crafting messages that resonate on a deeper level.
- **Use appropriate language:** The language you choose can either bridge gaps or create barriers. Choose language that is accessible and relatable to your audience, avoiding jargon or overly complex terms.

- **Adjust your delivery:** The way you deliver your message can be just as important as the message itself. Tailor your tone, pace, body language, and format to suit your audience, enhancing the impact of your message.
- **Be flexible:** Flexibility in communication means being willing to adjust your approach based on feedback and changing circumstances. Be adaptable in your communication approach, open to new ideas, and ready to adjust based on feedback and changing scenarios.

CASE STUDIES AND PRACTICAL EXERCISES

Let's look at two case studies that demonstrate the power of effective communication strategies in various contexts, from product launches and crisis management to space exploration and customer service.

Jeff Bezos, Founder of Amazon

At Amazon, Jeff Bezos recognized the limitations of traditional PowerPoint presentations in conveying complex information effectively. He saw a need for a more engaging and thorough approach to internal communications within the leadership team. Bezos implemented the use of detailed, narrative memos. These documents were meticulously prepared and shared before meetings. This approach required participants to engage deeply with the material beforehand, ensuring everyone had a comprehensive understanding of the topics to be discussed.

This shift led to more substantive and informed discussions among the team. It encouraged a culture of attention to detail and clear articulation of ideas, significantly improving the decision-making process. The emphasis on well-structured written communication not only made meetings more efficient but also fostered a deeper level of engagement and understanding across the leadership team.

Indra Nooyi, Former CEO of PepsiCo

Indra Nooyi's approach at PepsiCo highlights the significance of condensing complex ideas into clear, accessible messages. She faced the challenge of leading a diverse global team at PepsiCo, where conveying intricate business concepts in an accessible manner was critical for effective leadership.

Nooyi focused on distilling complex ideas into clear, relatable messages. She honed her communication skills to ensure that her messages were not only easy to understand but also resonated with a wide range of audiences within the company.

This approach significantly enhanced her ability to connect with and motivate her team. By simplifying complex concepts, Nooyi fostered a culture of clarity and accessibility in communication. This strategy was key in her successful leadership, demonstrating how effective communication can inspire and drive a diverse workforce toward common goals.

COMMUNICATION STYLE SELF-ASSESSMENT

To identify your communication style, take the following assessment. Your communication style could be based on well-known frameworks like assertive, passive, aggressive, and passive-aggressive styles.

Read each scenario and choose the response that best represents how you would typically behave in a professional setting. Be honest with yourself and select the option that most closely matches your usual communication style.

1. You're in a team meeting, and a colleague proposes an idea that you strongly disagree with. How do you respond?

A. Express your disagreement assertively, providing reasons for your stance.
B. Stay silent and avoid confrontation.
C. Immediately criticize the idea with strong words.
D. Make sarcastic remarks without directly addressing the idea.

2. Your team is working on a project, and you notice a mistake made by a colleague. How do you handle it?

A. Approach your colleague privately and offer constructive feedback.
B. Ignore the mistake and hope someone else notices it.
C. Publicly point out the mistake and blame your colleague.
D. Mockingly mention the mistake to others without talking to your colleague.

3. Your manager asks for your opinion on a new strategy. You have concerns but also see some potential benefits. What do you do?

A. Share your concerns and suggestions while acknowledging the strategy's merits.
B. Say you have no opinion to avoid any potential conflicts.
C. Criticize the strategy vehemently without offering alternatives.
D. Make passive-aggressive comments about the strategy without directly addressing it.

4. During a team brainstorming session, you have a unique idea that could change the project's direction. What's your approach?

A. Present your idea confidently, explaining its potential impact.

B. Keep your idea to yourself to avoid drawing attention.

C. Dismiss other ideas and insist on implementing your own.

D. Make subtle comments implying your idea is better without presenting it.

5. Your team is behind schedule on a project, and your manager is frustrated. How do you respond when asked about the delay?

A. Honestly explain the challenges and propose solutions.

B. Downplay the delay to avoid confrontation.

C. Blame team members for the delay and distance yourself.

D. Use humor to deflect blame without addressing the issue.

6. When receiving criticism from a colleague, how do you react?

A. Listen actively, ask for clarification, and consider their feedback.

B. Get defensive and dismiss their criticism.

C. Counterattack with criticism of your own.

D. Pretend to agree but later make passive-aggressive comments.

7. You have to delegate a task to a team member. How do you communicate your expectations?

A. Clearly outline the task, and expectations, and provide support if needed.

B. Avoid giving clear instructions to avoid conflicts.

C. Give vague instructions and expect them to figure it out.

D. Give instructions with a hidden agenda to create confusion.

8. When working on a group project, how do you handle disagreements with teammates?

A. Engage in open discussions to find common ground.
B. Avoid expressing your opinion to maintain harmony.
C. Dominate the discussion and insist on your viewpoint.
D. Use passive-aggressive comments to undermine opposing views.

9. You receive an email with a request that you find unreasonable. How do you respond?

A. Politely express your concerns and propose an alternative solution.
B. Ignore the email to avoid confrontation.
C. Respond with a strongly worded refusal.
D. Respond with passive-aggressive comments.

10. In a leadership role, how do you motivate your team to achieve a challenging goal?

A. Inspire and support your team, providing clear direction.
B. Avoid setting challenging goals to prevent stress.
C. Push your team aggressively to meet the goal, even if it leads to burnout.
D. Use sarcasm and humor to mock the goal without addressing it directly.

Scoring:

- A = Assertive
- B = Passive
- C = Aggressive
- D = Passive-Aggressive

Interpretation:

- Assertive communicators are open, honest, and respectful in their interactions, making them effective leaders.
- Passive communicators tend to avoid conflict but may struggle to assert themselves and lead effectively.
- Aggressive communicators can be dominating and confrontational, potentially harming team dynamics.
- Passive-aggressive communicators often use sarcasm and indirect comments, which can lead to misunderstandings.

In this chapter, we've embarked on a journey to enhance our communication skills, recognizing that effective communication is the cornerstone of successful leadership. We explored various aspects of communication, from understanding different communication styles to mastering the art of active listening.

Now that you have gained valuable insights into effective communication, it's time to put these ideas into action. Start by reflecting on your communication style and how it impacts your interactions with colleagues, team members, and superiors. Consider practicing active listening in your daily conversations, and don't shy away from providing constructive feedback when necessary.

As we polish our communication skills, we pave the way for stronger team dynamics. In the next chapter, "Building Strong Teams," we delve into how effective communication serves as the foundation for creating and nurturing high-performing teams. Get ready to explore the art of team building, where your newfound communication prowess becomes your greatest ally. We'll uncover strategies for fostering collaboration, resolving conflicts, and achieving outstanding results together.

So, stay tuned as we embark on the next leg of our leadership journey, where the power of effective communication will guide us toward building stronger and more successful teams!

CHAPTER 2
EMPOWER TEAMS:
SYNERGY IN TEAMWORK

"Alone we can do so little, together we can do so much."

HELEN KELLER

I n the journey of professional growth and achievement, one aspect stands as an undeniable truth: Teamwork is the bedrock upon which success is often built. Remember the last time you were part of a team that just clicked? Where every member was in sync, and the collective energy propelled you to achieve remarkable results? Now, imagine being the architect of such a team. This chapter unravels the blueprint of building strong, resilient teams that thrive on collaboration and shared success.

The goal of this chapter is to equip you with a profound understanding of the core principles of team dynamics and provide you with actionable strategies for fostering teamwork and collaboration. By the end of this chapter, you will have a clear grasp of how to build cohesive, high-performing teams and how to implement team-building activities effectively in your work environment. So, let's delve into the world of teamwork and unlock the secrets to success together.

FUNDAMENTALS OF TEAM DYNAMICS

So what makes a great team? A great team is not merely a collection of individuals working in the same vicinity; it is a dynamic entity that possesses a unique synergy, where the whole is greater than the sum of its parts. There are certain aspects of turning your team into a cohesive, high-performing unit.

- **Mutual respect:** One of the cornerstones of a successful team is mutual respect among its members. It's about recognizing the unique skills and perspectives each team member brings to the table. When team members respect one another, collaboration becomes more effective, fostering a positive work environment.
- **Specialization:** Great teams are composed of individuals with diverse skill sets. Each member brings their own expertise and

specializations to the group, contributing to a comprehensive skill pool that can tackle complex challenges effectively.

- **Defining purpose:** A shared and clearly defined purpose is vital for a team's success. When everyone understands their role in achieving a common goal, it becomes easier to align efforts and work toward a unified objective.
- **Adaptation:** In a dynamic work environment, adaptability is key. Successful teams can pivot when needed, responding to changes and challenges effectively. This flexibility ensures that the team can navigate unexpected situations with ease.
- **No scapegoats:** A great team operates on accountability. There are no scapegoats. Team members take responsibility for their actions, learn from their mistakes, and work together to find solutions.
- **Admit mistakes:** Mistakes are inevitable, but what sets great teams apart is their ability to acknowledge errors and learn from them. This culture of continuous improvement drives progress.
- **Patience:** Patience is a virtue, especially in a team setting. It's essential to recognize that achieving goals often takes time and perseverance. A patient team can overcome obstacles with determination.
- **Ability to delegate:** Effective delegation ensures that tasks are distributed based on individual strengths. Delegating responsibilities optimally is a sign of a well-organized team.
- **A strong leader:** While collaboration is key, a strong leader can provide guidance and direction when necessary. Effective leadership is instrumental in keeping the team on track and motivated.
- **Competitiveness:** Healthy competition within a team can drive members to perform at their best. It encourages innovation and continuous improvement.

In addition to these key factors, successful teams share several common traits, such as:

Successful Teams Communicate Well with Each Other

Effective communication is the lifeblood of any successful team. It goes beyond just exchanging words. Successful teams share ideas, feedback, and information in a clear and timely manner. Teams that communicate well have open channels where members listen actively, express themselves honestly, and value each other's perspectives. This approach fosters a sense of trust and camaraderie among team members, making it easier to collaborate and solve problems together. Effective communication ensures that everyone is on the same page, reducing misunderstandings and enhancing overall productivity.

They Focus on Goals and Results

Great teams are goal-oriented. They have a clear understanding of their objectives and a shared commitment to achieving them. These teams set Specific, Measurable, Attainable, Relevant, and Time-bound

(SMART) goals. By constantly focusing on these goals, team members stay motivated and aligned. They regularly assess progress and make necessary adjustments to ensure they are on the right track. This unwavering focus on results drives the team toward success and ensures that their efforts are purposeful and impactful.

Everyone Contributes Their Fair Share

In a high-performing team, every member actively contributes to the team's goals. This means that each individual takes responsibility for their assigned tasks and delivers them to the best of their abilities. Moreover, team members understand and appreciate the value of their unique skills and experiences, which they willingly share with the group. Contributions are not limited to the quantity of work but also encompass the quality of ideas, problem-solving, and creative input. A sense of shared ownership ensures that no one shirks their responsibilities and the workload is distributed equitably.

They Offer Each Other Support

Supportive team dynamics create a nurturing environment where members genuinely care about each other's well-being and success. In such teams, individuals are quick to offer assistance, guidance, and encouragement to their colleagues. This support extends beyond just work-related matters; it includes emotional support during challenging times as well. Knowing that they have a safety net of colleagues who genuinely care about their success, team members are more likely to take calculated risks, try new approaches, and ultimately achieve better results.

Team Members Are Diverse

Diversity within a team brings a wealth of perspectives, experiences, and ideas. Successful teams recognize the value of having members with different backgrounds, skills, and viewpoints. This diversity leads to more comprehensive problem-solving, increased innovation, and a broader range of solutions to challenges. It's essential to create an inclusive environment where everyone feels respected and heard, allowing the team to tap into the full potential of its diverse talents.

They Have Good Leadership

Effective leadership is the guiding force that ensures a team stays on course and thrives. A strong leader sets the vision, provides clear direction, and fosters a positive team culture. They lead by example, demonstrating the values and behaviors expected of team members. A good leader also empowers team members, encourages open communication, and makes decisions that benefit the team as a whole. Their ability to inspire and motivate is instrumental in achieving the team's goals.

They're Organized

Organizational skills are crucial for efficient teamwork. Organized teams have well-defined roles and responsibilities, clear processes, and streamlined workflows. This level of structure minimizes confusion and maximizes productivity. Members can focus on their tasks without being bogged down by administrative chaos. Organized teams are also better equipped to adapt to changing circumstances, as they have a solid foundation from which to work.

They Have Fun

While professionalism and dedication are paramount, having fun is an often overlooked yet essential aspect of a successful team. A positive and enjoyable work environment fosters enthusiasm, creativity, and a sense of belonging. Teams that enjoy their work tend to be more engaged, innovative, and resilient. Team-building activities, humor, and celebrating achievements together all contribute to a vibrant and enjoyable team culture.

The Importance of Diversity, Roles, and Personality Types in Teams

Diversity, roles, and personality types are integral components of successful team dynamics. Thoughtful allocation of roles ensures efficiency and minimizes conflicts. Ultimately, teams that excel in these areas are better positioned to achieve their goals and thrive in today's complex and ever-changing work environments.

Diversity

- Research, as mentioned in a Harvard Business Review article, has shown that diverse teams can lead to stronger financial performance. This positive outcome is because diverse teams bring a wider range of perspectives, ideas, and approaches to problem-solving, which can lead to better decision-making and innovation (Rock & Grant, 2016).
- Embracing diversity in teams expands the pool of available talent. It allows organizations to tap into a more extensive range of skills, experiences, and backgrounds, enhancing their ability to recruit and retain top talent.
- Diverse teams tend to make smarter decisions. When team members come from different backgrounds and possess varied viewpoints, they are more likely to consider a broader range of factors, leading to more informed and well-rounded decisions.
- Diversity fuels creativity and innovation within teams. It encourages members to think outside the box, challenge assumptions, and approach problems from different angles. This results in more effective problem-solving and a higher likelihood of finding novel solutions.
- Diverse teams are more likely to innovate. The collision of different ideas and perspectives often sparks creativity and the development of new products, services, or strategies.
- Inclusion and diversity can improve employee satisfaction and retention rates. When team members feel valued and included,

they are more likely to stay with the organization, reducing turnover costs.

Roles

- Team roles significantly influence how team members interact with each other. For example, a leader role might provide guidance and direction, while a coordinator role helps organize tasks and resources.
- Team roles contribute to the cohesion of the group. A well-balanced distribution of roles ensures that all essential functions are covered, reducing conflicts and misunderstandings.
- Different roles foster creativity by encouraging diverse thinking styles. For instance, an innovator role might bring fresh ideas, while a quality checker role ensures precision and accuracy.
- Effective team roles improve productivity by streamlining tasks and responsibilities. When each member knows their role and functions well within it, the team operates more efficiently.

Personality Types

- Just as individuals have personalities, teams develop collective personalities or dynamics. These dynamics influence how the team interacts, communicates, and makes decisions.
- Psychometric assessments can help identify the predominant personality preferences within a team. Understanding these preferences allows teams to adapt their communication and collaboration styles accordingly.
- The mix of personality types can impact team performance and job satisfaction. Teams that are aware of their collective personality tendencies can leverage strengths and address potential challenges proactively.

- Personality differences can lead to communication challenges and conflicts. By recognizing these differences and employing effective conflict-resolution strategies, teams can maintain harmony and productivity.

STRATEGIES FOR FOSTERING TEAMWORK AND COLLABORATION

Teamwork and collaboration are ongoing processes that require patience, dedication, and adaptability. There are some strategies that can pave the way for enhanced cooperation, productivity, and ultimately, the achievement of collective goals for you and your team:

- **Clarify all roles and responsibilities:** The foundation of effective teamwork begins with a clear understanding of each team member's role and responsibilities. This step involves delineating not just the overarching team goals but also the individual contributions required to achieve them. By creating a detailed roadmap of who does what, you minimize confusion, reduce overlapping efforts, and ensure that every team member knows their unique role in the collective effort.

- **Clarify goals and objectives:** Clearly defined goals and objectives act as the North Star guiding your team's journey. When everyone knows where they are heading and what they are striving to achieve, it fosters a sense of purpose and direction. Moreover, this clarity allows team members to align their efforts, resources, and decision-making toward common objectives, boosting overall productivity.

- **Let individuals use their best skills:** Each team member possesses a set of unique skills and talents. Encouraging individuals to leverage their strengths not only contributes to the team's success but also fosters a sense of fulfillment and engagement. This approach recognizes that diversity in skills enriches the team's collective capabilities, leading to more innovative problem-solving and improved outcomes.

- **Set clear rules:** Rules and guidelines provide the necessary structure for effective collaboration. Clear and well-communicated rules of engagement can prevent misunderstandings, reduce conflicts, and ensure a smoother workflow. These rules may cover aspects like meeting protocols, communication methods, and task allocation, creating a reliable framework for teamwork.

- **Cultivate thinking as a team:** A hallmark of successful teams is their ability to brainstorm and make decisions collectively. Encouraging open discussions and idea sharing fosters an environment where diverse perspectives can flourish. By valuing and integrating contributions from every team member, you promote innovation and inclusive decision-making.

- **Encourage the team to hold each other accountable:** Accountability is the cornerstone of trust within a team. Encourage team members to not only take ownership of their tasks but also support one another in fulfilling their commitments. This mutual accountability strengthens the team's bond and ensures that everyone remains dedicated to achieving shared goals.

- **Engage the team in group decision-making:** Inclusive decision-making empowers team members and fosters a sense of ownership over the outcomes. Engaging the entire team in significant decisions not only taps into their collective wisdom but also cultivates a culture of shared responsibility, where everyone feels valued and involved.
- **Address problems as they occur:** Conflict and challenges are inevitable in any collaborative endeavor. The key is to address them promptly and constructively. Encourage open communication to identify issues early on, and implement effective conflict resolution strategies to maintain a healthy team dynamic.
- **Sponsor team building activities:** Team building activities go beyond icebreakers and trust falls; they create lasting bonds among team members. Plan activities that promote camaraderie, trust, and a deeper understanding of each other's strengths and weaknesses. These activities can include team lunches, outdoor adventures, or even volunteering together.
- **Engage the team in brainstorming together:** Collective brainstorming sessions can yield innovative ideas that may not have surfaced through individual efforts. Create an environment where team members feel comfortable sharing their thoughts and encourage them to build upon each other's ideas. This collaborative approach often leads to breakthrough solutions and increased creativity.
- **Reward strong team performance:** Recognizing and rewarding exceptional team performance reinforces the importance of collaboration and motivates continued excellence. Celebrate achievements as a team, whether through verbal praise, bonuses, or other incentives. Acknowledgment goes a long way in boosting team morale and dedication.
- **Focus on effective communication:** Effective communication is the glue that holds all these strategies together. Encourage open, transparent, and consistent

communication among team members. Foster a culture where questions are welcomed, feedback is constructive, and information flows freely, ensuring that everyone stays informed and aligned.

The Role of Trust and Transparency in Building Effective Teams

Trust and transparency stand in team dynamics and guide the way toward unprecedented productivity and collaboration. It makes every team member feel valued, understood, and secure in expressing their true selves and ideas.

- **Trust builds psychological safety:** A study by Google identified psychological safety as the most crucial factor for team success (Bariso, 2018). This concept, as Timothy R. Clark of LeaderFactor explains, is rooted in the predictability of behavior within a team. High trust levels encourage members to engage and participate without fear of embarrassment or retribution, fostering an environment where people feel safe to express themselves (*Timothy R. Clark Psychological Safety*, n.d.).
- **Trust encourages questioning:** In environments where trust is lacking, team members often hesitate to ask questions due to fear of seeming incompetent or disruptive. This fear can lead to poor decision-making and misunderstandings. Conversely, when trust is present, questioning leads to clarification, better decisions, and ultimately, enhanced results.
- **Trust creates goodwill (and minimizes miscommunications):** Trust shapes how we interpret and respond to communications. In low-trust settings, a simple message can be misconstrued, leading to conflicts. Trust acts as a buffer, allowing team members to assume positive intentions and resolve misunderstandings more amicably.

- **Trust encourages innovation and rapid decision-making**: High-trust environments are conducive to innovation and quick decision-making. They create a safe space for risk-taking, which is essential for innovation. In such environments, there's less second-guessing, and teams can move swiftly and confidently.
- **Trust enhances morale:** Teams with high levels of trust tend to have more fun and be more effective. This dynamic is particularly true in high-stakes environments like the military or law enforcement, where trust is crucial for survival. High morale in trusting teams leads to better long-term results and less dysfunction.

TEAM BUILDING ACTIVITIES AND THEIR REAL-WORLD APPLICATIONS

Team building activities are crucial in fostering strong relationships within a team. Let's explore a range of team-building exercises and the objectives they can help you accomplish:

- **Breed loyalty:** Team-building activities can instill a sense of loyalty among employees. They help individuals feel connected to the organization, fostering a deeper commitment to its goals and values.
- **Share company culture:** These exercises provide a platform for sharing and reinforcing your company's culture. They allow employees to experience firsthand the core principles and beliefs that drive your organization.
- **Save money:** It may seem counterintuitive, but team-building can lead to cost savings in the long run. By improving collaboration and communication, teams can work more efficiently, reducing operational expenses.
- **Foster employee bonds:** Strengthening interpersonal relationships within the team is a primary goal. These activities help break down barriers and create stronger bonds among team members.

- **Encourage communication:** Effective communication is the backbone of any successful organization. Team-building exercises provide opportunities to enhance communication skills, ensuring that messages are clear and understood.
- **Build skills:** Team-building activities can serve as a training ground for skill development. Whether it's leadership, problem-solving, or creativity, these exercises offer a practical platform for honing various abilities.
- **Teach conflict prevention and resolution:** Conflict is inevitable in any workplace, but how it's managed can make all the difference. Team-building exercises often simulate challenging situations, allowing participants to practice conflict prevention and resolution techniques.
- **Unite a virtual workforce:** With the rise of remote work, uniting a dispersed workforce is essential. Team-building activities can bridge the geographical gap and create a sense of unity among virtual teams.

Some effective communication-based team-building activities include these six examples:

1. **Coffee chats:** This activity involves randomly pairing two team members for a relaxed conversation over coffee. It's an excellent way for colleagues to share their interests and personal life, enhancing mutual understanding and camaraderie. This activity can be adapted for remote teams using video conferencing tools.
2. **Scavenger hunts:** This activity requires teamwork and communication as employees work together to find items or complete tasks. It's engaging and can be easily set up in the office environment, fostering a spirit of collaboration and problem-solving.
3. **The question ball:** A simple yet effective activity where a beach ball with questions written on it is tossed among team members. The catcher answers the question nearest to their

right thumb, encouraging open communication and personal sharing.

4. **Two truths and a lie:** Each team member presents three "facts" about themselves, with one being a lie. The group then guesses the lie. This game is a fun way to learn more about each other and encourages openness in a light-hearted manner.

5. **Board games:** Playing board games is a classic team-building exercise. It brings team members together in a relaxed setting, promoting interaction, strategic thinking, and team spirit.

6. **Blindfolded obstacle course:** Pairs navigate an obstacle course with one blindfolded and the other giving verbal directions. This activity enhances trust and communication skills, as the blindfolded person must rely on their partner's guidance.

How to Tailor These Activities to Different Types of Teams and Settings

Tailoring team-building activities to different types of teams and settings involves several important considerations:

- **Know your audience:** It's essential to understand the composition and dynamics of your team. Consider their preferences, backgrounds, and experiences to ensure the activities are inclusive and engaging for everyone.
- **Define your objectives:** Clearly identify what you want to achieve with your team-building program. Your desired outcomes could range from improving communication and fostering psychological safety to enhancing problem-solving skills or creativity.
- **Choose your format:** Decide whether the activities will be in-person, virtual, or hybrid. This choice should reflect the current working environment of your team and the nature of the activities planned.

- **Select your activities:** Choose activities that align with your objectives and are suitable for your team's composition. These are great for establishing a foundation for cross-functional teams, where understanding roles and creating a safe environment for diverse opinions is crucial.
- **Facilitate with skill:** Effective facilitation is key to the success of team-building activities. The facilitator should guide the process, encourage participation, and ensure that the objectives of the activity are met.

CASE STUDIES SHOWING THE IMPACT OF THESE ACTIVITIES ON TEAM PERFORMANCE

Team building activities have shown significant positive impacts on team performance in various organizations:

Bill and Melinda Gates Foundation "Bookworm Builders" Event

- **Situation/task:** The Bill & Melinda Gates Foundation identified the need for a unique charity initiative that would foster team collaboration and make a meaningful impact on the community.
- **Action:** They organized "Bookworm Builders," a charity event where participants could work together creatively. The event involved teams assembling and decorating bookshelves, which were then filled with books and donated to under-resourced schools and libraries.
- **Result:** This innovative approach not only enhanced team collaboration and bonding but also had a tangible positive effect on the community. The bookshelves provided much-needed resources to educational institutions, reinforcing the Foundation's commitment to learning and development.

Principia's Engagement with Outback Team Building & Training

- **Situation/task:** Principia, grappling with the challenge of building a cohesive company culture in a remote working environment, recognized the need for a strategic intervention.
- **Action:** They enlisted Outback Team Building & Training to conduct an Emotional Intelligence training session. The session included activities and discussions designed to enhance emotional awareness and empathy among employees, fostering a deeper understanding of each other's experiences and perspectives.
- **Result:** The training had a profound impact, leading to improved alignment with the company's values and a more connected workforce. The success of this initial session prompted Principia to schedule ongoing sessions, cementing the training's role in nurturing a more empathetic and cohesive remote working culture.

TEAM BUILDING ACTIVITY PLANNER

To plan and execute a successful team-building session, follow these steps:

1. **Define objectives:** Identify specific goals for the team-building activity. Are you aiming to improve communication, trust, problem-solving skills, or just having fun?
2. **Choose the right activity:** Based on your objectives, select an activity that aligns with your goals. Consider the interests and physical capabilities of your team.
3. **Budgeting:** Establish a budget that includes costs for the venue, food, transportation, and the activity itself.
4. **Schedule and venue:** Selecting the right date and venue is key for team-building events. Aim for a time when workloads are light, and choose a venue that's different from the usual

workspace, whether it's offsite or a unique spot within the office. An ideal venue acts as neutral ground, encouraging openness and vulnerability among team members. This shift away from the familiar not only breaks down formalities and encourages free thinking but also promotes a sense of interdependence and trust, which are vital for effective team bonding and collaboration.

5. **Communication:** Inform your team about the details of the event well in advance. Include the purpose, expectations, and any preparations they need to make.
6. **Prepare materials:** Ensure all necessary materials and equipment for the activity are ready.
7. **Execution:** On the day, lead the activity, keeping engagement and energy levels high. Be adaptable to any changes or challenges.
8. **Debriefing:** After the activity, have a debriefing session to discuss learnings and observations. Relate the experience back to workplace scenarios.
9. **Feedback and follow-up:** Collect feedback from participants to gauge the session's effectiveness and plan for future improvements.

In this comprehensive chapter, we've navigated the intricate world of team-building exercises, uncovering their diverse objectives and the profound impact they can have on your organization. Now, it's time to put these ideas into action. Consider the specific objectives you aim to achieve within your organization and select team-building exercises that align with those goals. Encourage your team to participate actively and wholeheartedly, as the benefits will extend far beyond the activity itself.

Now, with a strong team foundation in place, it's time to sharpen another crucial skill in leadership: decision-making. In the next chapter, "Decision-Making in Leadership," we delve into the art of making informed, timely decisions. This chapter will guide you in mastering decision-making skills that distinguish great leaders, propelling your team toward remarkable achievements. Get ready to explore how to make choices that align with and advance your team's goals.

CHAPTER 3
ANALYZE AND DECIDE: STRATEGIC DECISION-MAKING

"Not making a decision is actually a decision. It's the decision to stay the same."

LYSA TERKEURST

I magine standing at a crossroads where one decision can alter the course of your team and your career. This situation isn't just about choosing right or wrong; it's about making decisions with confidence and clarity. In this chapter, we dissect the anatomy of decision-making in leadership, turning what often feels like a gamble into a calculated, strategic move.

Leadership is not about merely occupying a position; it's about actively shaping the path ahead. As you delve into the content of this chapter, you will undergo a transformation in your approach to decision-making. We aim to shift your perspective from one of anxiety to one of strength.

By the end of this chapter, you will possess a profound understanding of various decision-making frameworks. You'll learn how to strike the delicate balance between intuition and analysis, and most importantly, you'll gain the confidence to tackle high-stakes decisions with poise.

FRAMEWORKS FOR EFFECTIVE DECISION-MAKING

Decision-making is a skill that can greatly impact the success of any leader. It involves more than just choosing between options; it's about systematically analyzing situations, predicting outcomes, and selecting the best course of action. This process is where decision-making models and frameworks come into play. They provide structured approaches to navigate complex scenarios, allowing leaders to break down problems, evaluate alternatives, and make choices that are not just reactive but strategically sound. These models enhance clarity, reduce bias, and promote a more thoughtful consideration of various factors and potential impacts. These frameworks help leaders ensure their decisions are consistent, rational, and aligned with their objectives and values. There are six main kinds of decision-making models:

- **Rational Decision-Making Model**

This model follows a logical, structured approach. It starts with defining the problem, setting criteria, weighting these criteria, generating alternatives, evaluating them, and finally selecting and implementing the best solution. This model is ideal when there are multiple options and sufficient time for evaluation.

- **Bounded Rationality Decision-Making Model**

Here, the focus is on finding a "good enough" solution quickly, rather than the best possible one. This model is suitable in situations where time is a critical factor and swift action is required.

- **Vroom-Yetton Decision-Making Model**

This model is unique in its approach, offering a decision tree based on seven yes/no questions. It's particularly effective in collaborative settings, helping leaders determine the extent of team involvement in decision-making.

- **Intuitive Decision-Making Model**

This model relies on a leader's instincts and experience, especially when there's limited information or the need for quick decisions.

- **Recognition Primed Model**

Similar to intuitive decision-making, this model also depends on the leader's experience but includes a step to visualize potential outcomes of various solutions.

- **RAPID Decision-Making Model**

Developed by Bain & Company, this model clarifies decision accountabilities among multiple stakeholders. It's a structured approach that defines the roles in the decision-making process: Recommend, Agree, Perform, Input, and Decide. This model is effective in reducing ambiguity and streamlining the decision-making process.

Decision-Making Frameworks for Individual and Collective Contexts

There are some differences between lone decision-making and collective decision-making frameworks.

Lone Decision-Making Frameworks

Sometimes, as a manager, you may need to make decisions independently. Here are three frameworks that can assist you in making solitary decisions effectively:

- **CSD Matrix:** This framework (Certainties, Suppositions, Doubts) helps organize information into categories of certainty and uncertainty.
- **Golden Circle:** Introduced by Simon Sinek, this model focuses on the "why: at its core, surrounded by the "how" and the "what" of decision-making.
- **Decision Graphs:** Utilizes graphical representations to assess the importance of various options based on their connections to objectives and other options.

Collective Decision-Making Frameworks

Collaborative decision-making is another critical aspect of leadership. Here are three frameworks designed for collective decision-making scenarios:

- **RICE/ICE:** These are prioritization frameworks that are useful in making collective decisions by assigning values to Reach, Impact, Confidence, and Ease (or Effort). Scoring each of these factors on a scale can help you calculate a priority score for tasks or projects, helping you decide which ones to tackle first.
- **Decision Trees:** This framework offers a visual representation of potential outcomes of decisions, facilitating group understanding and consensus.
- **Multi-vote, Multi-veto:** This framework engages groups in voting for and against options, fostering a consensus-driven approach to decision-making.

Incorporating these frameworks and skills into your management repertoire can significantly enhance your effectiveness as a leader, equipping you to make well-informed decisions that align with your team's goals and organizational objectives. Each framework offers unique insights and methods, making them invaluable tools in a leader's skill set.

Now, let's explore various decision-making models that you as a manager can apply in different leadership scenarios. These models include:

- **Rational Model:** This model is best suited for situations where there is clarity of information and the problem is well-defined. It's ideal for strategic planning and complex problem-solving where risks and outcomes can be analyzed thoroughly. For instance, in a corporate restructuring scenario, you can use this model to weigh different restructuring strategies against set criteria to make an informed decision.

- **Intuitive Model:** This model is applicable in fast-paced environments where quick decisions are essential, and there's not enough time for a thorough analysis. Leaders with extensive experience in a particular field can rely on their instincts to make decisions. For example, if you are a startup CEO, you can use this model when deciding to pivot the business direction based on market feedback.

- **Recognition-Primed Model:** This model is a blend of intuition and analysis, suitable for emergency or high-pressure situations. It's particularly effective for leaders with deep experience in a specific area. For instance, a firefighter chief might use this model to quickly assess a rapidly evolving situation and make life-saving decisions.

- **Vroom-Yetton Model:** This model is geared toward decision-making in a team or group context. It helps determine the level of team involvement in decision-making. In a scenario where a new product is being developed, a manager might use this model to decide how much input to seek from the team regarding features and design.

- **Bounded Rationality Model:** This model is useful in scenarios where time, information, and cognitive limitations are factors. Leaders recognize that they can't analyze every piece of information and instead make the best decision possible with the available information. This model is often used in high-stress business environments, like stock trading, where decisions need to be made rapidly with incomplete information.

- **Creative Model:** This model is ideal for scenarios that require innovative and out-of-the-box thinking, often in marketing, product development, or problem-solving in new markets. A leader using this model might facilitate brainstorming sessions to encourage creative solutions to a market entry strategy.

BALANCING INTUITION AND ANALYSIS

Leadership often requires a harmonious blend of intuition and analysis. Intuition, the innate "gut feeling," plays a pivotal role in decision-making. However, relying solely on intuition can lead to biased or uninformed decisions. Conversely, an overemphasis on data and analysis can lead to paralysis by analysis, where decisions are delayed due to excessive information processing. This section explores the importance of striking a balance between these two elements.

The Importance of Balancing Gut Feelings With Factual Analysis

Effective leaders understand the value of aligning their instinctual insights with empirical data. Gut feelings are inherently subjective and can be influenced by personal experiences and biases. However, they are also rapid and adaptive, offering immediate guidance in uncertain situations. On the other hand, factual analysis provides an objective foundation for decisions, ensuring they are grounded in reality and not just personal beliefs.

Harvard Business published an article, *Data, and Intuition: Good Decisions Need Both*, that emphasizes the synergy between intuition and data in effective decision-making. It discusses how relying solely on data can sometimes lead to decision paralysis, especially when data quality is low or overwhelming. Contrarily, intuition, particularly in critical decisions, acts as a valuable complement to data. The article cites Google's Project Oxygen as an example, showing how qualitative data on staff performance and satisfaction led to better management practices. Understanding and assessing emotions can clarify decision-making processes. This concept is central to effective leadership, especially in terms of integrating both analytical and instinctive approaches (Farrell, 2023).

Practical Examples of Balancing Intuition and Analysis

Let's look at some practical scenarios where leaders successfully balanced their intuition with data. One such example is a company committed to employee well-being. In this scenario, a company faces a decision about its healthcare benefits. The data indicates that eliminating these benefits would save money. However, the company is committed to its employees' well-being, a core part of its ethos. This situation exemplifies the tension between data-driven decisions and the company's values. While the data suggests a cost-saving measure, acting on this alone would contradict the company's fundamental commitment to employee welfare. It illustrates the necessity for leaders to weigh both hard data and the organization's core values and mission in their decision-making process, rather than relying solely on quantitative analysis.

Key Strategies for Leaders

Effective decision-making requires leaders to:

- **Evaluate the situation in its entirety:** Leaders must take a holistic view of every decision-making scenario, considering all factors, including those that are not immediately quantifiable.
- **Analyze potential solutions informed by experience, data, and feedback:** It's crucial for leaders to draw on their own experiences, seek diverse perspectives, and incorporate data-driven insights to explore different solutions.
- **Align decisions with core values, goals, and mission statements:** Decisions should consistently reflect the organization's foundational principles. This alignment ensures that even difficult decisions contribute positively to the organizational culture and long-term objectives.

How Intuition and Analysis Have Played a Role in Key Business Decisions

Intuition and analysis play pivotal roles in shaping key business decisions. Successful leaders and entrepreneurs have often shared their experiences and insights on how these two elements intertwine. Let's delve into some examples and ideas (*What Are Some Examples of Successful Leaders*, n.d.):

- **Steve Jobs's unwavering trust in intuition:** Steve Jobs, the co-founder of Apple, was a firm believer in the power of intuition. He famously advised, "Don't let the noise of others' opinions drown out your own inner voice." He emphasized the importance of having the courage to follow your heart and intuition. This approach guided him in making groundbreaking decisions that transformed Apple into a tech giant.
- **Oprah Winfrey's intuitive wisdom:** Media mogul and philanthropist Oprah Winfrey has credited her success to her trust in the "still, small voice of intuition." She has openly admitted that her only mistakes occurred when she didn't listen to her intuition. Oprah's ability to connect with her audience and make impactful decisions reflects the influence of intuition in her career.
- **Jeff Bezos and gut instinct:** Jeff Bezos, the founder of Amazon, believes that some of his most significant decisions were not driven by data analysis but rather by "heart, intuition, and guts." This sentiment underscores the idea that intuition can complement and sometimes surpass rigorous analysis in making critical business choices.
- **Angela Merkel's creative problem solving:** Angela Merkel, the former chancellor of Germany, emphasizes the role of intuition and creativity in solving complex problems. She recognizes that intuition, combined with analytical thinking,

can lead to innovative solutions when facing challenges in the political arena.

These examples showcase how intuition and analysis can coexist in the decision-making process of successful leaders. It's a delicate balance that allows leaders to harness the power of their intuition while being informed by data and analysis to navigate complex business landscapes.

Tips on Developing Both Intuitive and Analytical Skills

Developing both intuitive and analytical skills is crucial for a well-rounded approach to decision-making. Here are some tips on how to nurture these skills:

Developing Intuitive Skills:

- **Practice mindfulness:** Developing your intuition involves tuning in to your inner voice and paying attention to the signals it sends you. Mindfulness techniques, such as meditation or simply being present in your daily activities, can help you become more in touch with your intuition. To achieve this outcome, you will want to set aside time to quiet your mind and reflect on your thoughts and feelings.

- **Seek feedback:** It's essential to gather feedback from various sources, including mentors, peers, customers, or anyone who can provide constructive and honest input. Other people can offer different perspectives and insights that can help you better understand your own intuitive tendencies.
- **Experiment and take calculated risks:** To enhance your intuition, be willing to experiment with it. This experimentation could involve testing your assumptions, trying new approaches, and taking calculated risks in your decision-making. This process allows you to gain experience and learn from both successful outcomes and failures.
- **Learn from others:** Observing and learning from the intuition of others, especially experienced leaders, can be incredibly valuable. Study how they rely on their intuition in various situations, and seek to understand the thought processes behind their decisions.
- **Reflect on successes and failures:** Regularly reflect on your own successes and failures in decision-making. Understand what factors led to positive outcomes and what contributed to any setbacks. Learning from your experiences helps refine your intuitive judgment over time.

Developing Analytical Skills:

- **Enhance decision-making:** Focus on enhancing your decision-making skills by developing a structured approach to problem-solving. Analyze data, assess risks, and consider various scenarios before making choices.
- **Let go of structure (sometimes):** While analytical thinking is crucial, it's also essential to know when to let go of rigid

structures. Be open to creative and intuitive solutions that may not fit into a conventional analytical framework.

- **Improve communication:** Effective communication is a vital part of analytical leadership. Learn to convey complex analytical findings in a clear and understandable manner to team members and stakeholders.
- **Embrace teamwork:** Encourage collaboration and teamwork within your organization. Diverse perspectives and collective analytical thinking can lead to more robust and well-informed decisions.
- **Maintain productivity:** Analytical leaders should balance thorough analysis with the need for timely decisions. Strive to maintain productivity by setting realistic deadlines and focusing on the most critical aspects of a problem.

By consciously working on both your intuitive and analytical skills, you can become a more well-rounded leader capable of making informed and innovative decisions in various situations.

HIGH-STAKES DECISIONS TRAPS

There are mainly five high-stakes decision-making traps. Let's explore these five traps in more detail:

1. **The Anchoring Trap:** In high-stakes decision-making, people can become anchored to a single piece of information or a particular course of action. This occurs when individuals rely too heavily on the first piece of information they receive, which can lead to a skewed perspective. To avoid this trap, decision-makers should seek a broad range of information sources and remain open to adjusting their views as more data becomes available.

2. **The Status-Quo Trap:** The status-quo trap occurs when decision-makers default to maintaining the current situation because it feels comfortable or familiar. High-stakes situations

often demand change and adaptation. Falling into this trap can lead to missed opportunities or inadequate responses to challenges. To overcome it, decision-makers must actively question the status quo and be willing to consider innovative solutions.

3. **The Sunk-Cost Trap:** The sunk-cost trap involves making decisions based on the amount of time, effort, or resources already invested, rather than evaluating the decision's future potential. High-stakes decisions should focus on the expected benefits and risks moving forward, rather than being influenced by past investments. Decision-makers should be ready to cut their losses when necessary.

4. **The Confirming Evidence Trap:** People tend to seek out information that confirms their existing beliefs or preferences while ignoring or downplaying contradictory evidence. In high-stakes situations, this confirmation bias can lead to suboptimal decisions. Decision-makers should actively seek out diverse perspectives and evidence, even if it challenges their preconceived notions.

5. **The Framing Trap:** The framing trap occurs when decision-makers are influenced by how a problem or decision is presented, rather than objectively evaluating the core issues. The way a situation is framed can impact the perception of risks and benefits. To avoid this trap, decision-makers should reframe problems in different ways to gain a more comprehensive understanding.

Handling High-Stakes Decision Traps

Recognizing and avoiding these traps is crucial for making well-informed and effective high-stakes decisions. When confronted with high-pressure decisions that carry significant consequences, a well-structured approach is vital to ensure the best possible outcome. Here's an in-depth exploration of strategies for effectively navigating high-stakes situations:

- **Clear your mind:** The first step in handling high-stakes decisions is to create mental clarity, which involves freeing your mind from distractions and emotions that may cloud your judgment. High-stakes decisions require a calm and focused mindset. Take a few moments to practice mindfulness techniques, such as deep breathing or meditation, to center yourself and gain clarity.
- **Determine the desired outcome:** Clearly defining the desired outcome is paramount. This involves specifying what you aim to achieve with your decision. A well-defined outcome serves as a guiding light, helping you stay on course amidst uncertainty. Consider the long-term goals and overarching objectives that your decision should align with.
- **Prioritize key factors:** High-stakes decisions often involve complex factors that can overwhelm even the most seasoned professionals. To navigate this complexity, identify and prioritize the critical factors that will have the most significant impact on the decision's outcome. Focus your attention and resources on these key variables while avoiding distractions from less relevant details.
- **Make decisions intuitively:** Trusting your intuition can be a valuable asset in high-stakes situations. Your intuition, honed through experience and knowledge, often provides valuable insights that complement analytical reasoning. Embrace your gut feeling, but balance it with data and logic to ensure a well-rounded decision-making process.
- **Prepare for potential consequences:** Every decision carries consequences, both positive and negative. In high-stakes scenarios, it's crucial to anticipate and prepare for potential outcomes. Develop contingency plans and strategies to address a range of possible consequences. This proactive approach minimizes surprises and enhances your ability to adapt.
- **Weigh decisions against probability and desirability:** Evaluate potential outcomes by considering both their probability and desirability. This dual assessment helps you

make decisions based on a realistic understanding of the likelihood of various results and the impact they would have on your goals and objectives.

- **Understand the problem:** Gain a deep and comprehensive understanding of the problem at hand. High-stakes decisions often involve multifaceted issues that require thorough analysis. Invest time in gathering relevant information, conducting research, and seeking expert opinions to ensure you grasp the nuances of the situation.
- **Utilize decision matrices:** Decision matrices provide a systematic framework for evaluating and comparing different options. Create a matrix that includes key criteria and assign scores or weights to each criterion. This structured approach facilitates a more objective assessment of your alternatives.
- **Weigh the need for more data with the timing:** Balancing the need for more data with the urgency of the decision is a critical aspect of high-stakes decision-making. Evaluate whether waiting for additional information is worth the delay. Consider the impact of timing on your goals and whether the data you anticipate gathering will significantly change the decision's outcome.
- **Break problems down into basic elements:** Complex problems can become more manageable when you break them down into smaller, more manageable components. Analyze and address each element individually, gradually building a comprehensive solution. This approach prevents you from feeling overwhelmed and helps maintain clarity.
- **Brainstorm pros and cons:** Employ the classic technique of brainstorming the pros and cons of each available option. This visual method allows you to weigh the advantages and disadvantages of different choices systematically. It also encourages creative thinking and a comprehensive assessment of potential outcomes.

- **Recognize and evaluate your assumptions:** Acknowledge your assumptions and biases in the decision-making process. Challenge them and ensure they align with the facts and data available. Seek diverse perspectives and actively consider alternative viewpoints to mitigate the impact of cognitive biases.

Maintaining Clarity Under Pressure

Leadership stress is unique due to the complex blend of challenges and responsibilities that come with leadership roles. It often stems from balancing multiple demands, such as achieving goals, managing conflicts, and carrying the weight of responsibility. Recognizing the nature and causes of this stress is crucial for effective management. Here are some ways you can work under pressure:

- **Know what's causing stress:** Begin by identifying the sources of stress in your life. Explore the underlying causes and triggers of your stress to address them effectively. Awareness is the first step toward managing stress.
- **Stop perfectionism in its tracks:** Perfectionism can be a major source of stress. Instead of aiming for perfection, strive for excellence. Understand that mistakes and imperfections are part of growth and learning. Allow yourself some flexibility and self-compassion.
- **Ask for and accept support:** Don't hesitate to seek support from colleagues, friends, or a mentor. Sharing your challenges and concerns with others can provide valuable insights and emotional relief. It's a sign of strength, not weakness, to ask for help when needed.
- **Practice time management:** Effective time management can reduce stress. Prioritize tasks, create schedules, and set clear goals. Break your workload into manageable chunks and allocate time for important activities. Time management helps you stay organized and in control.

- **Delegate out duties:** As a leader, it's crucial to delegate tasks and responsibilities to team members. Trust your team to handle certain responsibilities, freeing up your time and mental bandwidth for critical decisions. Delegation also empowers your team and fosters their growth.
- **Take enough breaks:** Don't underestimate the importance of breaks. Regular short breaks during work can improve productivity and reduce stress. Step away from your tasks, take a walk, practice deep breathing, or engage in quick relaxation exercises to refresh your mind.
- **Make healthy diet changes:** Nutrition plays a significant role in managing stress. Incorporate a balanced diet rich in fruits, vegetables, whole grains, and lean proteins. Avoid excessive caffeine and sugar, which can contribute to stress and anxiety.
- **Get plenty of sleep:** Quality sleep is essential for mental clarity and stress management. Aim for seven to nine hours of restful sleep each night. Establish a consistent sleep routine and create a comfortable sleep environment to improve sleep quality.

In addition to the strategies mentioned, it's essential to proactively address your mental and emotional well-being. Consider practices like mindfulness meditation, deep breathing exercises, or engaging in hobbies that bring you joy and relaxation. These activities can help you stay grounded and maintain clarity under pressure.

Leadership through Camaraderie–Luis Urzúa

In 2010, a catastrophic collapse at the San Jose copper-gold mine in northern Chile trapped 33 miners 700 meters underground. In this dire situation, foreman Luis Urzúa emerged as a remarkable leader. Recognizing the gravity of the accident, Urzúa immediately assumed leadership and organized the trapped men for an extended survival ordeal.

What sets Urzúa's leadership apart is his ability to foster camaraderie and mental resilience among the miners. He played a crucial role in maintaining their spirits and mental well-being throughout the harrowing 70-day ordeal. Urzúa also took practical steps by creating detailed maps of the mine to assist with the rescue effort and closely coordinating with engineers on the surface.

Luis Urzúa's story serves as a powerful example of leadership under extreme pressure. His ability to maintain composure, provide emotional support, and collaborate effectively with experts led to the eventual rescue of all 33 miners. His leadership was a beacon of hope and solidarity in one of the most challenging situations imaginable.

This story reminds us that effective decision-making and leadership shine brightest in times of crisis. They inspire us to persevere, innovate, and prioritize the well-being of those we lead, even when faced with the most daunting challenges.

REFLECTIVE JOURNAL

Creating a reflection journal can be a powerful tool for personal growth and learning. Here are some prompts that can guide you in reflecting on your decisions:

1. Describe a recent decision:

- What was the decision you had to make?
- What factors did you consider before making this decision?

2. Explore the outcomes:

- What were the results of your decision?
- How did it affect you and others involved?

3. Assess your decision-making process:

- Did you feel you had enough information to make an informed choice?
- Were there any biases or emotions that influenced your decision?

4. Reflect on the learning experience:

- What did you learn about yourself through this decision-making process?
- How has this decision impacted your understanding of effective decision-making?

5. Consider alternative approaches:

- Looking back, were there other options you could have considered?
- How might these alternatives have changed the outcome?

6. Plan for future decisions:

- What strategies can you adopt to improve your decision-making in the future?
- Is there a particular aspect of decision-making you want to develop or improve upon?

At the heart of it, decision-making is a complex and intricate process, akin to a dance of critical choices made under varying degrees of pressure. This chapter took us on a journey through the experiences of leaders who, in their defining moments, faced uncertainty at these crossroads and emerged victoriously. Their stories act as guiding lights, showing us the way in our own decision-making journeys.

As we delve deeper into the art of decision-making, it's important to acknowledge that this journey isn't always smooth. Conflicts, both internal and external, are an integral part of the decision-making process. Chapter 6 delves into the heart of these conflicts, examining how they arise and, more importantly, how they can be navigated. We'll explore strategies to resolve conflicts, ensuring they become constructive elements that enrich, rather than hinder, the decision-making process. Chapter 6 promises to equip you with the tools to turn conflicts into catalysts for making more informed, balanced decisions.

As we move on to the next chapter of our journey, prepare to dive into the heart of leadership: the art of cultivating relationships. In the upcoming chapter, titled "Cultivating Relationships," we'll unveil the profound impact that strong connections can have on effective leadership. From elevating team morale to shaping the outcomes of your decisions, these relationships are the cornerstone of your leadership prowess. Get ready to unravel the secrets behind building enduring and influential connections that will redefine your leadership journey.

CHAPTER 4
DEVELOP RELATIONSHIPS: TRUST AND NETWORK BUILDING

"Good teams become great ones when the members trust each other enough to surrender the 'me' for the 'we'."

PHIL JACKSON (NBA COACH)

Consider the strongest leaders you know. What sets them apart? Often, it's their ability to forge powerful connections. This chapter is about turning interactions into lasting relationships and transforming acquaintances into allies. It's where leadership transcends the boundaries of mere management and becomes a journey of meaningful connections.

In the realm of effective leadership, one pivotal truth shines through: the indispensable role of building relationships. As we embark on this chapter, we're delving deep into the core of leadership, unveiling the essential role that nurturing professional networks plays in steering leaders toward success.

Our objective within these pages is crystal clear—to emphasize the significance of cultivating professional connections. By the end of this journey, you will grasp the utmost importance of constructing trust and rapport. You'll witness firsthand how these skills wield a direct and profound impact on your journey as a leader.

THE POWER OF RELATIONSHIP-BUILDING

The power of relationship-building cannot be underestimated. It is the cornerstone upon which successful leadership is built, and it is a force that has the potential to transform not only leaders themselves but also the organizations they guide.

Relationship-building plays a pivotal role in leadership. Here, we'll explore why it holds such paramount importance:

- **Fosters trust:** Building relationships fosters trust among team members, which is a crucial element in any leadership equation. Trust is the bedrock upon which strong teams and successful leaders stand.

- **Enhances communication:** Effective communication thrives within well-forged relationships. It's through these bonds that leaders can convey their visions and ideas clearly and persuasively.
- **Encourages collaboration:** When relationships are nurtured, collaboration becomes not just a possibility but a natural outcome. Leaders can harness the collective strength of their teams.
- **Inspires team loyalty:** Leaders who invest in relationships earn the loyalty of their team members. Loyalty, in turn, leads to commitment and dedication.
- **Facilitates effective decision-making:** Strong relationships enable leaders to seek and receive valuable input from their teams, facilitating sound decision-making.
- **Promotes innovation:** In an environment where relationships thrive, individuals feel safe to share innovative ideas, driving the organization forward.
- **Increases employee engagement:** Engaged employees are a product of positive relationships. Leaders who prioritize this engagement reap the benefits of a motivated workforce.
- **Enhances problem-solving capabilities:** When faced with challenges, leaders with well-established relationships can tap into a network of problem-solving resources.
- **Builds a strong organizational culture:** Relationships shape the culture of an organization, fostering an environment of collaboration, inclusivity, and shared values.
- **Ensures sustainable success:** Ultimately, it's the strength of relationships that ensures the sustainable success of leaders and organizations alike.

Understanding the value of strong professional relationships is even backed by compelling statistics and research. These insights underscore the significance of fostering connections in the workplace (May, 2023a):

- **Eighty percent of employees between the ages of 18 and 24 years old would be happier if they felt more connected with their colleagues. However, only 47% of employees over 54 years old feel the same way.** This statistic showcases how different age groups value workplace relationships and their impact on overall happiness.
- **Nearly three in five (57%) people say working alongside someone who they consider a friend makes work more enjoyable. Meanwhile, around 21% believe it positively impacts how productive and creative they feel.** These percentages illustrate how friendships at work can enhance both the enjoyment and productivity of employees.
- **More than a third of employees said that they have never spent time with their manager outside of work; however, 70% of them said they would actually want to.** This data highlights the potential for stronger manager-employee relationships and their positive impact on workplace dynamics.

There are many stories that collectively underscore a critical aspect of leadership—that success often hinges not just on individual capabilities, but also on the strength and quality of one's networks.

Let's discuss the case study of the Colorado Department of Transportation (CDOT). Under the leadership of Gary Vansuch and Michelle Malloy, CDOT successfully integrated a Change Agent Network, significantly enhancing their organizational efficiency and effectiveness.

This network was carefully constructed with individuals selected for their emotional intelligence and ability to influence, rather than their hierarchical positions. The core of this initiative was to foster trust, confidence, and engagement across various levels of the organization. Vansuch and Malloy's strategy involved in-depth training on human behavior during times of change, ensuring that each member was equipped to facilitate and advocate for new initiatives.

The structure of CDOT's network, encompassing regional offices yet functioning as a unified entity, serves as an exemplary model. It demonstrates how formalizing such networks can create a robust framework for change, backed by executive support and an emphasis on training. This model shows that leadership success in today's dynamic environment hinges on the ability to create, nurture, and utilize networks of change agents effectively.

NURTURING PROFESSIONAL NETWORKS

Nurturing professional networks has become an indispensable skill for managers and executives alike. This section delves into the practical strategies and insights you need to expand and maintain your professional networks effectively.

- **Joining a networking group:** Discover how connecting with like-minded professionals in dedicated networking groups can open doors to new opportunities and insights.

- **Utilizing social media:** Explore the power of social platforms as tools for expanding your network in the digital age.
- **Growing a database of professional contacts:** Learn how to curate and maintain a robust database of contacts to ensure your network remains dynamic and relevant.
- **Joining industry groups:** Understand the significance of industry-specific associations and groups in forging meaningful connections.
- **Attending conventions and conferences:** Discover how these events can serve as fertile grounds for networking and knowledge exchange.
- **Sending emails:** Learn the art of staying in touch with your contacts through personalized and meaningful emails.
- **Setting up informational interviews:** Explore how informational interviews can not only strengthen your relationships but also provide you with valuable insights.
- **Offering assistance:** Understand the significance of being a resourceful and supportive member of your professional community.

Strategies for Networking in Various Settings

Networking is a vital skill that can open doors to new opportunities, foster professional relationships, and enhance your career prospects. Networking encompasses a diverse range of scenarios, both in-person and online. To excel in this endeavor, it's essential to adapt your approach to different settings. Here's a breakdown of key strategies:

- **Prepare ahead:** Before any networking event, virtual or physical, meticulous preparation is key. Research the attendees, set clear goals, and have your elevator pitch ready. This groundwork will boost your confidence and effectiveness.
- **Present yourself well:** Your initial impression matters immensely. Dress professionally, maintain good posture, and

project confidence. A polished appearance and demeanor can leave a lasting positive impression.

- **Always be ready to give your pitch:** Craft a concise and engaging elevator pitch that highlights your strengths and what you bring to the table. Be ready to deliver it seamlessly when the opportunity arises.
- **Ask questions and listen actively:** Effective networking is not just about talking; it's also about listening. Show genuine interest in others by asking questions and actively engaging in conversations. This approach demonstrates your willingness to learn and collaborate.
- **Ask for help:** Don't hesitate to seek assistance when needed. Networking is a two-way street, and offering help and requesting it can strengthen connections.
- **Expand your online presence:** In the digital age, a robust online presence is crucial. Maintain professional profiles on platforms like LinkedIn, Twitter, and other relevant social media sites. Share valuable content and engage with your network regularly.
- **Be conscious of your digital image:** Your online persona matters. Ensure that your digital footprint reflects your professionalism and expertise. Regularly review and curate your online content to align with your career goals.
- **Do your research:** Before connecting with someone, conduct thorough research. Understand their background, interests, and current endeavors. This knowledge can help you initiate meaningful conversations.
- **Stay in touch with your network:** Networking is an ongoing process. Regularly reach out to your connections to stay updated on their progress and share yours. Consistent communication fosters strong relationships.
- **Grow your network:** Seek opportunities to expand your network continually. Attend industry events, conferences, and webinars, and join relevant online communities. Building a diverse network can open doors to unforeseen opportunities.

- **Pursue your hobbies:** Networking doesn't always have to revolve around work. Pursue your hobbies and interests, as they can lead to unexpected connections and shared passions.
- **Attend webinars:** Participating in webinars relevant to your field is an excellent way to network. These virtual events often attract like-minded professionals and provide opportunities for meaningful interactions.
- **Start a podcast:** Creating a podcast can establish you as an authority in your field. Invite industry experts and thought leaders as guests to build your network and share valuable insights.

Balancing Professional Boundaries With Personal Connections

Now that we've explored strategies for effective networking, let's delve into the delicate art of balancing professional boundaries with personal connections. Navigating this aspect of your career with finesse is essential for maintaining both your work relationships and personal life harmoniously. Here's some valuable advice:

- **Limit socializing with colleagues:** While it's essential to foster positive relationships with colleagues, it's equally crucial to set limits on socializing. Avoid excessive mingling during work hours and ensure you maintain a clear separation between your professional and personal life.
- **Avoid gossip and negativity:** Gossip and negative conversations can erode trust and damage professional relationships. Refrain from engaging in or perpetuating such discussions. Instead, focus on constructive conversations that contribute positively to the workplace.
- **Be aware of power dynamics:** In any professional setting, power dynamics exist. Be mindful of these dynamics and strive to treat all colleagues with respect and fairness, regardless of their position within the organization. Avoid exploiting personal connections for professional gain.

- **Communicate clearly and respectfully:** Effective communication is the linchpin of maintaining healthy boundaries. Clearly communicate your expectations and boundaries to colleagues and friends in the workplace. Approach difficult conversations with respect and empathy to preserve relationships.

TECHNIQUES FOR BUILDING TRUST AND RAPPORT

Building trust is like laying a strong foundation, and fostering rapport is akin to constructing the walls of a harmonious working relationship. Together, these elements form the framework for collaboration, effective communication, and a supportive work environment.

In this section, we will explore proven techniques and strategies designed to empower you in the realm of trust and rapport. These techniques will not only enhance your professional interactions but also elevate your overall effectiveness in the workplace.

- **Recognize that building trust takes hard work:** Understand that trust is not easily gained; it's a valuable commodity that requires continuous effort. Acknowledge the importance of investing time and energy into building trust with colleagues and associates. Trust is a fundamental building block for successful working relationships.
- **Be honest and supportive:** Honesty forms the bedrock of trust. Be forthright in your communication with colleagues, and avoid misleading or concealing information. Provide support when needed. Demonstrating your willingness to help and support others, whether professionally or personally, fosters a sense of trust and reliability.
- **Be transparent:** Openness and transparency are essential in building trust. Share information openly, including both positive and negative aspects. Be honest about your intentions and actions, ensuring that colleagues can rely on you to

communicate openly and honestly. This transparency cultivates trust.

- **Seek First to Understand and Then Be Understood:** This approach emphasizes the value of empathetic listening—understanding others' perspectives before expressing your own. This approach fosters effective communication and stronger relationships, as it ensures that all parties feel heard and valued. By prioritizing understanding, one can communicate their own views more effectively, leading to more meaningful and productive interactions.
- **Be consistent:** Consistency in your actions and behavior is key to building trust. Colleagues should know what to expect from you. Maintaining a predictable and reliable demeanor helps build trust over time, as it demonstrates your commitment to your principles and values.
- **Model the behavior you seek:** Lead by example. Demonstrate the qualities and behaviors you wish to see in others. Your actions set the standard for trust and rapport in the workplace. When you exhibit integrity, respect, and professionalism, you inspire others to do the same, creating a culture of trust.
- **Build in accountability:** Hold yourself accountable for your commitments and responsibilities. When you consistently follow through on your promises and demonstrate accountability for your actions, others are more likely to trust your word and actions. Accountability builds credibility.
- **Extend empathy to others:** Empathy is a crucial element in building rapport and trust. Take the time to understand and acknowledge the feelings and perspectives of your colleagues. Show genuine care for their well-being and experiences. Empathy enhances emotional connections.
- **Solicit feedback and take action on suggestions:** Actively seek input from your colleagues and be open to their feedback. When you demonstrate a willingness to listen and act on suggestions for improvement or change, it conveys your

commitment to collaboration and continuous improvement, earning trust in the process.

- **Demonstrate appreciation:** Regularly express gratitude and appreciation for the efforts and contributions of your colleagues. Acknowledging the hard work and dedication of others fosters positive relationships and trust. Small gestures of appreciation can go a long way in building trust and rapport in the workplace.
- **Praise the work of others publicly and privately:** Acknowledging the achievements and contributions of your colleagues, both in public forums and private conversations, reinforces their value and strengthens bonds.
- **Show a genuine interest in others and ask the right questions:** Taking a sincere interest in your colleagues' lives and aspirations fosters a deeper connection. Asking thoughtful questions demonstrates your commitment to understanding them better.
- **Establish equally important values to create common goals:** Aligning your values and goals with those of your colleagues fosters a sense of unity. When everyone shares a common purpose, trust and rapport naturally flourish.

Exercises and Prompts to Practice These Techniques

To truly master the techniques for building trust and rapport, it's crucial to put them into practice in real-world scenarios.

Real-World Application of Rapport-Building Questions

The art of question-asking is indeed a potent tool for building rapport, and its effectiveness lies in its simplicity and genuine intent. When you incorporate questions like, **"What brings you here today?"** or, **"What can I do to make your day better?"** into your interactions, you're doing more than initiating a conversation. These questions serve as catalysts for deeper engagement, signaling your willingness to understand and cater to the needs or interests of the other person.

Consider the subtle yet profound impact of a question like, "**Is this the first time you've tried something like this?**" This query not only opens up a dialogue about the other person's experiences but also provides insights into their comfort level and expectations. It shows that you are interested in their story, their challenges, and their journey.

Similarly, when you ask, "**Do you think there's anything I can do to make this easier for you?**" you're extending a hand of support. It's an invitation for the other person to share their concerns or needs, creating a space where vulnerability is met with empathy. This level of attentiveness can transform a simple interaction into a moment of true connection.

Questions like, "**What are you hoping this will lead to?**" or, "**How does this compare to your last experience?**" encourage the other person to reflect and share their aspirations and reflections. Such questions demonstrate that you value their perspective and are interested in what drives them, what disappoints them, and what they aspire to achieve.

Each of these questions, framed in the right tone and context, acts as a step toward a more meaningful and connected dialogue. They help peel away the layers of superficial interaction, revealing the common human desire to be understood and appreciated. In the realm of professional and personal relationships, mastering these questions is not just about skillful conversation. It's about fostering an environment of trust, respect, and mutual understanding, which are the cornerstones of lasting and meaningful connections.

S-CONNECT: A Guiding Framework for Building Rapport

Embrace the S-CONNECT acronym as your compass in the journey of building rapport. It stands for:

- **S**tay in the present moment: Focus fully on the interaction, letting go of distractions.
- **C**reate open body language: Your physical stance can speak volumes about your openness and willingness to engage.
- **O**bserve non-verbal cues: Much of communication is non-verbal. Pay attention to these silent signals.
- **N**otice what your "gut" tells you: Intuition often provides clues about the underlying dynamics of an interaction.
- **N**urture the conversation: Cultivate the dialogue with care, showing interest and encouragement.
- **E**ngage with eye contact: It's a simple yet profound way to establish a connection.
- **C**onvey warmth with your voice tone: The way you speak can either build bridges or walls.
- **T**alk less, listen more: Encourage the other person to share, creating a space where they feel heard and valued.

TRUST-BUILDING EXERCISES

In the journey of cultivating a harmonious team environment, trust-building exercises play a pivotal role. These exercises are the stepping stones toward creating a culture of mutual respect, understanding, and collaboration.

- **The trust fall:** A classic yet powerful exercise. Team members take turns falling backward, trusting that another member will catch them. This exercise, although simple, requires a great deal of trust in team members and helps in breaking down barriers of doubt and apprehension.

- **Two truths and a lie:** A light-hearted yet revealing game where each member states two truths and one lie about themselves, and others guess which is the lie. This activity encourages attentiveness and offers insights into each other's lives, fostering a deeper personal connection.
- **Blindfolded obstacle course:** Team members guide a blindfolded colleague through a simple obstacle course. This exercise emphasizes the importance of clear communication and trust in each other's instructions, enhancing team coordination.
- **Reflection sessions:** Regularly scheduled sessions where team members share their thoughts on what they appreciate about each other, challenges faced, and feedback. This practice nurtures an environment of open communication and mutual respect.
- **Joint problem-solving tasks:** Engaging the team in problem-solving activities where they must work together to find a solution. This group activity not only promotes teamwork but also reinforces trust in each other's abilities and judgment.

Each of these exercises, though differing in nature, serves a common purpose: to fortify the foundation of trust and rapport within a team. It's important to approach these activities with a sense of openness and willingness to engage. The ultimate aim is to cultivate stronger mutual trust and understanding within the team.

Remember, the essence of these exercises lies in their consistent application and the sincerity with which they are approached. As trust within the team grows, so does the potential for collective success.

As we draw this chapter to a close, let's take a moment to reflect on the key takeaways and the significant strides we've made in understanding the intricate art of building trust and rapport. We've uncovered the profound impact of skillful question-asking, delving into how it opens doors to deeper understanding and connection. We've also navigated through various trust-building exercises, each designed to fortify the bonds within a team, reinforcing the significance of mutual respect, clear communication, and collaboration.

Now, it's time to bring these insights to life. I encourage you to not just read about these techniques but to actively implement them in your daily interactions. Whether it's through a thoughtful question or a team-building exercise, each step you take is a move toward stronger, more meaningful relationships. Remember, the true value of these lessons lies in their application. As you practice, you'll not only see a transformation in your interactions but also in the overall dynamics of your team or personal relationships.

Looking ahead, our journey through the realms of effective leadership and relationship management takes an exciting turn. As we master the art of cultivating relationships, we pave the way for another crucial aspect of leadership: motivation. In Chapter 5, we discuss the strategies that transform leaders into sources of inspiration for their teams. This chapter promises to be a captivating exploration of how motivation acts as the driving force behind a team's success. Get ready to explore how motivation can be the driving force behind your team's success.

CHAPTER 5
STIMULATE MOTIVATION: INSPIRING TEAM EXCELLENCE

"Teamwork is the foundation of success. The three universal questions that an individual asks of his coach, player, employee, or employer are: Can I trust you? Are you committed to excellence? And, do you care about me?"

LOU HOLTZ

Have you ever wondered why some teams buzz with energy and drive while others seem to trudge along? The secret lies in motivation. This chapter isn't just about encouraging your team; it's about unlocking their potential and igniting a passion that leads to extraordinary results.

Theories and ideas alone are insufficient without practical application. This chapter goes beyond theory, offering you actionable insights into implementing successful motivation strategies. You will gain the know-how to translate your newfound understanding into tangible results, elevating team productivity and bolstering morale to unprecedented heights.

So, if you're eager to unlock your team's hidden potential, if you aspire to lead a team that not only meets but surpasses expectations, then join me as we unravel the intricate web of team motivation and ignite a passion for extraordinary results.

UNDERSTANDING WHAT DRIVES MOTIVATION

Understanding what drives motivation in a team is essential for any leader or manager aiming to foster a high-performing and engaged workforce. Digging deeper into the essence of motivation, leaders and managers must grasp not just the *how* but the *why* of team and individual motivation. Understanding the intrinsic reasons why team members do what they do, what drives their dedication, and why they choose to contribute their talents in this specific environment is key. This process involves exploring their personal goals, aspirations, and values. It's about connecting their individual *why* to the broader objectives and culture of the organization. This deeper under-standing enables leaders to tailor their approach, ensuring that moti-vational strategies resonate on a more personal and impactful level. Aligning organizational goals with individual aspirations allows leaders to foster a more motivated, committed, and purpose-driven team.

Several motivational theories are particularly relevant to team dynamics, providing a structured framework to understand and apply these concepts effectively:

- **Maslow's Hierarchy of Needs** is a fundamental theory in understanding human motivation. It's structured as a pyramid, starting with basic physiological needs at the bottom and culminating in self-actualization at the top. In a team context, this theory suggests that leaders should aim to fulfill the varying needs of their team members, recognizing that these needs can be met simultaneously at different levels. For example, ensuring a safe and comfortable working environment addresses physiological and safety needs while recognizing achievements and providing opportunities for growth can fulfill esteem and self-actualization needs.
- **Herzberg's Two-Factor Theory**, another pivotal concept, distinguishes between hygiene factors (like salary and work conditions) that prevent dissatisfaction and motivators (like recognition and responsibility) that truly drive satisfaction and motivation. This theory underscores the importance of not only addressing basic needs but also providing elements that genuinely inspire and energize team members.
- **McClelland's Theory of Needs** focuses on three primary drivers: the need for achievement, the need for affiliation, and the need for power. Understanding these needs helps in tailoring motivational strategies according to the individual preferences and drives of team members.
- **Expectancy Theory** emphasizes the role of expectations in motivation, proposing that individuals are motivated when they believe that their efforts will lead to desirable outcomes. This theory highlights the importance of setting clear goals and ensuring that the rewards are aligned with these goals.

- **Goal-setting Theory** suggests that specific, challenging goals enhance team motivation and performance. It emphasizes the importance of setting clear, achievable objectives and providing feedback on progress.

Factors That Influence Motivation in the Workplace

Building upon our exploration of motivational theories, it's crucial to discuss the various factors that influence motivation in the workplace. These factors are multifaceted and interact in complex ways to shape an employee's experience and drive. Let's delve into these key elements:

- **Leadership:** The style and quality of leadership within an organization significantly impact employee motivation. Effective leaders inspire, guide, and support their teams, creating an environment where employees feel valued and motivated.
- **Organizational culture:** The culture of a company, defined by its values, norms, and practices, greatly influences

motivation. A positive, inclusive, and supportive culture can boost morale and motivation, whereas a negative culture can have the opposite effect.

- **Paths to advancement:** Clear opportunities for advancement within the organization encourage employees to stay motivated and engaged. Knowing there is a path forward fosters a sense of purpose and ambition.
- **Professional development Opportunities:** Access to training and development programs shows employees that the organization is invested in their growth, which can be a powerful motivator.
- **Recognition:** Acknowledging employees' hard work and achievements is vital. Recognition, whether through verbal praise, awards, or promotions, boosts morale and encourages continued high performance.
- **Work environment:** The physical work environment, from comfortable office spaces to remote work flexibility, can significantly affect motivation levels. A pleasant and adaptable work environment contributes to employee satisfaction and productivity.
- **Flexibility:** Offering flexibility in work arrangements, such as remote working options or flexible hours, can lead to increased motivation by accommodating employees' varying needs and lifestyles.
- **Belonging:** Fostering a sense of belonging within the team or organization enhances motivation. When employees feel like they are a valuable part of a community, they are more likely to be engaged and committed.
- **Work/life balance:** Maintaining a healthy balance between professional and personal life is crucial for motivation. Overwork and stress can lead to burnout, whereas a balanced approach boosts morale and productivity.
- **Meaningful work:** Engaging in work that feels meaningful and impactful can greatly motivate employees. When people

see the value and purpose in their work, they are more likely to be committed and driven.

- **Salary and non-monetary incentives:** While salary is a fundamental motivator, non-monetary incentives such as acknowledgment of extraordinary performance, recognition of achievements, and efforts to create a positive work environment also play a crucial role.
- **Relationships in the workplace:** Both relationships with colleagues and leadership are pivotal. A positive and supportive network within the organization fosters a sense of community and belonging.
- **Company's culture and internal processes:** The overall culture of the company, along with its internal processes, shapes the daily experiences of employees, influencing their motivation.
- **Personal life:** An employee's personal life and circumstances can also impact their motivation at work. Acknowledging and supporting this aspect can lead to a more motivated workforce.
- **Performing meaningful work:** Similar to meaningful work, employees are motivated when they feel their work has a significant impact and contributes positively to the organization or society.

Understanding the psychological and management perspectives on the drivers of motivation in the workplace enriches our grasp of this complex yet vital aspect of team dynamics. Insights from various studies reveal a multifaceted view of what propels employees toward engagement and high performance.

A key aspect is the concept of meaningful work. Research demonstrates that when employees perceive their work as meaningful, it positively correlates with enhanced work engagement and overall performance. This relationship is mediated by factors such as the use of personal strengths and work engagement, highlighting that meaningful work contributes to performance in several interrelated ways.

It's not just about the task at hand but how the work aligns with an employee's values and sense of purpose (Van Wingerden & Van der Stoep, 2018).

Psychological studies also emphasize the importance of understanding individual motivations and strengths. The perception of meaningful work varies among individuals, and this subjective assessment can significantly influence whether employees feel motivated and engaged. This underscores the value of recognizing and supporting each team member's unique strengths and motivations (Pappas, 2021).

Moreover, the environment in which employees work plays a crucial role. A supportive work environment that acknowledges and fosters the use of individual strengths can lead to increased motivation. This involves not just the physical workspace but also the interpersonal dynamics, organizational culture, and the recognition of individual contributions.

These insights align with broader motivational theories, such as Maslow's Hierarchy of Needs and Herzberg's Two-Factor Theory, by emphasizing the need for a holistic approach to employee motivation. It's about creating a balance between meeting basic needs and providing opportunities for growth, recognition, and meaningful engagement (*The Psychology of Employee Motivation*, 2023).

Implementing these insights requires a nuanced understanding of both individual and collective needs within a team. It involves creating an environment that not only addresses basic physiological and safety needs but also fosters a sense of belonging, acknowledges individual achievements, and supports personal and professional growth.

TECHNIQUES FOR INSPIRING AND MOTIVATING TEAM MEMBERS

To inspire and motivate team members effectively, you can employ a range of strategies. These techniques are designed not only to boost morale and productivity but also to foster a supportive and engaging work environment.

- **Set clear goals and share them with your team:** Establishing clear, achievable goals is fundamental. This step provides direction and purpose, allowing team members to align their efforts toward common objectives. This clarity helps in driving focus and motivation.
- **Give team members autonomy:** Trust is a cornerstone of motivation. Allowing team members the autonomy to make decisions and take ownership of their tasks empowers them, fostering a sense of responsibility and self-motivation.
- **Accommodate flexible work schedules:** Acknowledging the diverse needs of your team members, such as work-life balance, can significantly boost motivation. Offering flexible work schedules demonstrates your commitment to their well-being and can enhance overall job satisfaction.
- **Encourage open and frequent communication:** Regular and transparent communication helps build trust and ensures everyone is on the same page. It allows for the sharing of ideas, feedback, and concerns, thereby creating a collaborative atmosphere.
- **Balance workload among team members:** Ensuring a fair distribution of work prevents burnout and maintains high morale. It's important that team members feel their workload is manageable and fair.
- **Give and receive feedback:** Constructive feedback is a two-way street. Regularly providing feedback and actively seeking input from team members not only improves performance but also strengthens motivation through a sense of continuous improvement.
- **Recognize and reward contributions:** Acknowledgment and appreciation go a long way in motivating a team. Recognize and reward their efforts, whether through praise, bonuses, or other incentives, to reinforce their sense of achievement.
- **Invest in professional development:** Offering opportunities for professional growth shows that the organization is invested

in the future of its employees. This can include training programs, workshops, or educational resources.

- **Create a welcoming and comfortable workspace:** The physical environment can significantly impact motivation and productivity. A comfortable, well-equipped workspace can make a big difference in how team members feel about their work.
- **Engage in team-building activities:** Regular team-building activities help in fostering camaraderie and a sense of belonging, which are key to a motivated team.

A crucial aspect of effective team motivation lies in the art of personalization. Understanding what motivates each team member individually can have a profound impact on engagement, trust, growth, and performance.

- **Increase engagement:** When you tailor your motivational strategies to each team member's unique preferences and aspirations, you create a level of engagement that transcends the ordinary. Engaged team members are more committed and enthusiastic about their work, resulting in increased productivity and job satisfaction.
- **Build trust:** Personalized motivation communicates that you value and respect each team member as an individual. This foundation of trust is vital in fostering open communication and collaboration. Team members are more likely to trust a leader who understands their needs and desires.
- **Foster growth:** Every team member possesses distinct ambitions and areas for growth. By acknowledging and addressing these specific aspirations, you enable personal and professional development that aligns with their goals. This not only motivates but also contributes to long-term career satisfaction.
- **Enhance performance:** The direct impact of personalized motivation on performance cannot be overstated. When team

members feel that their efforts are recognized and rewarded in a way that resonates with them personally, they are more likely to excel in their roles, contributing to the overall success of the team.

REAL-LIFE EXAMPLES OF SUCCESSFUL MOTIVATION STRATEGIES

Moving beyond the theoretical framework of motivational theories, let's look at the real world and examine how effective motivation strategies have yielded remarkable results for leaders and their teams. These real-life success stories underscore the importance of motivation in team dynamics. They showcase the tangible benefits of motivation strategies, such as increased productivity, improved morale, and the successful completion of projects.

Transformation at Google

In a landmark study featured in The New York Times, Google embarked on a quest to build the perfect team. By implementing motivation strategies that emphasized psychological safety, equal participation, and fostering a sense of belonging, they achieved remarkable outcomes. Teams became more innovative, creative, and productive, demonstrating the tangible benefits of motivational strategies in the workplace (Duhigg, 2016).

The Power of Recognition at Boeing

Boeing, a giant in the aerospace industry, recognized the significance of acknowledging employees' contributions. Through a well-designed recognition program, Boeing not only increased employee morale but also witnessed significant improvements in productivity and project completion rates. This case study, documented in scholarly articles, illustrates the transformative power of recognizing and celebrating team achievements (Thornton, 2021).

Leading with Empathy at Apple

Apple, under the leadership of Tim Cook, demonstrated the profound impact of empathetic leadership. By understanding employees' individual needs and aspirations, Cook inspired a sense of purpose and dedication within the team. This approach resulted in heightened motivation, increased job satisfaction, and a surge in innovative product developments (Steinmann et al., 2019).

MOTIVATIONAL QUOTES AND REFLECTIONS

Incorporating motivational quotes and reflections into your leadership approach can be an inspiring and thought-provoking element. These quotations, drawn from the wisdom of various leaders and thinkers, can offer valuable insights and serve as prompts for reflection on your leadership style and practices.

Ronald Reagan: "The greatest leader is not necessarily the one who does the greatest things. He is the one that gets people to do the greatest things."

- Consider a time when you empowered your team to achieve remarkable things. How did you facilitate their success?

Simon Sinek: "Leadership is not about being in charge. It is about taking care of those in your charge."

- Reflect on how you've supported your team's growth and well-being. What steps can you take to enhance their experience?

Peter F. Drucker: "Management is doing things right; leadership is doing the right things."

- Think about a difficult decision you had to make. How did you balance efficiency with ethical considerations?

John C. Maxwell: "A leader is one who knows the way, goes the way, and shows the way."

- How do you lead by example in your organization? In what ways could you improve your approach?

Steve Jobs: "Innovation distinguishes between a leader and a follower."

- Consider how you encourage innovation within your team. What strategies can you implement to foster more creative thinking?

In summary, this chapter has been a journey into the heart of team motivation, unveiling the theories and strategies that underpin the drive for excellence within your team. We've explored the intricacies of Maslow's Hierarchy of Needs, Herzberg's Two-Factor Theory, McClelland's Theory of Needs, Expectancy Theory, and Goal-Setting Theory. Additionally, we've delved into real-life examples that demonstrate the transformative power of motivation in the workplace.

Looking ahead, our journey continues in the next chapter. While motivating your team lays the foundation for success, it's equally vital to navigate the complexities of conflict and change. In the next chapter, we will explore how effective leaders turn challenges into opportunities and foster a resilient and adaptable team environment. Prepare to learn the art of transforming obstacles into stepping stones, as we equip you with the skills to lead your team through the dynamic landscape of change and conflict, ultimately propelling your team toward unprecedented success.

UNLOCK THE POWER OF GENEROSITY

"The best way to find yourself is to lose yourself in the service of others."

MAHATMA GANDHI

People who give without expecting anything back live longer, happier lives and make more money. So,if we can do that while we learn together, I'm all for it.

To do that, I have a question for you...

Would you help someone you've never met, even if you never got credit for it?

Who is this person you ask? They are like you. Or, at least, like you used to be. Less experienced, wanting to be a better leader, and needing help, but not sure where to start.

Our mission is to make effective leadership skills accessible to everyone. Everything we do comes from that mission. The only way for us to achieve that mission is by reaching...well...everyone.

This is where you come in. Most people do, in fact, judge a book by its cover (and its reviews). Here's my ask on behalf of a struggling manager you've never met:

Please help that manager by leaving this book a review.

Your gift costs no money and less than 60 seconds to make real but can change a fellow manager's life forever. Your review could help...

...one more team work together better. ...one more leader communicate more clearly. ...one more manager make smarter decisions. ...one more colleague build stronger relationships. ...one more leader grow and improve.

To get that 'feel good' feeling and help this person for real, all you must do is...and it takes less than 60 seconds... leave a review.

Simply scan the QR code below to leave your honest feedback on Amazon. Thank you for your generosity and support!

Thank you!

Thank you!

CHAPTER 6
TACKLE CONFLICTS: ADAPTIVE CONFLICT MANAGEMENT

"I don't think anyone ever gets completely used to conflict. If it's not a little uncomfortable, then it's not real. The key is to keep doing it anyway."

PATRICK LENCIONI

I n the life of every leader, there comes a moment when a sudden conflict or an unexpected change tests their mettle. How you respond in these moments can define who you are as a leader. This chapter isn't just about resolving conflicts; it's about turning them into opportunities for growth and mastering the art of adaptability.

In the world of leadership, there arises a pivotal juncture—a moment that challenges the very essence of one's capabilities. When unforeseen conflicts erupt or unexpected changes unfold, a leader's mettle is put to the test. It is in these defining moments that the true character of leadership shines through. This chapter embarks on a profound journey, one that transcends the mere resolution of conflicts; it is a voyage into the realm of transformation and an exploration of adaptability as the cornerstone of effective leadership.

Our journey through this chapter will provide you with insights, wisdom, and practical guidance to not only resolve conflicts effectively but also to embrace change as an ally rather than an adversary. By the chapter's end, you will be equipped with the knowledge and tools to fortify your leadership, fostering a resilient and thriving team under your guidance.

WHY CONFLICT RESOLUTION IS IMPORTANT

Why does understanding the root cause hold such significance? As a new manager, one of the most daunting challenges you might face is conflict management within your team. It's a common concern, under-scored by statistics that show a significant portion of an employee's time in the UK and the US is spent dealing with interpersonal conflicts. Notably, conflicts can account for up to 40% of a manager's time (Laker & Pereira, 2022).

The shift to remote and hybrid work environments has further compli-cated the landscape, making conflict harder to identify and address. However, conflict isn't inherently negative. It can prevent complacency and stimulate innovative thinking.

Conflict management is a critical skill often overlooked in leadership training, and poor handling of conflicts can impact team dynamics and your reputation as a manager. The key is to learn how to effectively mitigate and manage conflicts, turning challenges into opportunities for team growth and development. There are many factors as to why it is important:

- **In-depth investigation:** Delving into the underlying issues of a conflict requires a thorough investigation. This investigation often involves open-ended questioning and active listening to uncover deeper grievances or misunderstandings.
- **Visual mapping techniques:** Tools like the cause and effect diagram (fishbone diagram) are instrumental in visually organizing the various factors contributing to a conflict. This method allows for a comprehensive view of potential causes, leading to more targeted solutions.
- **Psychological factors:** Often, team conflicts stem from underlying emotional or psychological factors, such as perceived disrespect or unaddressed past grievances. Acknowledging and addressing these factors is vital for true resolution.
- **Long-term solutions:** By identifying root causes, resolutions can be more sustainable, preventing the recurrence of similar conflicts.
- **Team development:** Understanding and resolving these root causes not only solves immediate problems but also contributes to the overall development and cohesion of the team.

APPROACHES TO CONFLICT RESOLUTION

Effective conflict resolution is essential in any workplace, and there are various techniques to achieve this outcome.

Addressing the Conflict

Leadership often presents situations where conflicts arise, and addressing them promptly becomes a critical task. The first step in this process is to recognize these conflicts early and approach them with a constructive mindset. It's not just about acknowledging that a problem exists; it's about getting ready to deal with it in a way that promotes positive outcomes.

Clarifying the Issue

To effectively navigate conflicts, it's essential to gain a deep under-standing of the root causes behind them. Clarifying the issue at the heart of the conflict involves more than just scratching the surface. It requires thorough investigation and fact-finding, all while being an attentive and impartial listener. It's crucial to avoid hasty judgments based on incomplete or biased information.

Bringing the Parties Together

With a clearer understanding of the conflict's intricacies, you must take on the role of mediator, orchestrating a conducive environment for open communication. Bringing the involved parties together to talk is a pivotal moment in the conflict resolution journey. Here, you act as a guardian of constructive dialogue, ensuring that the exchange remains respectful, focused, and solution-oriented. In this controlled setting, each party is granted the opportunity to express their viewpoints, free from the chaos of miscommunication and misunderstanding.

Identifying a Solution

Moving forward, the focus shifts to finding a resolution that everyone involved can agree upon. This stage isn't about winning or losing; it's about fostering collaboration and seeking solutions that benefit all parties. It often involves compromise and the pursuit of a "win-win" outcome where everyone's needs and objectives are considered.

Monitoring and Long-Term Efficacy

Even after a resolution has been reached, the journey is far from over. The commitment to conflict resolution extends into the realm of monitoring and follow-up. Leaders must periodically check in to ensure that the agreed-upon solution is being adhered to and remains effective over time. This vigilance ensures that conflicts do not resurface and that the team continues to function harmoniously.

Investigating the Broader Context

In some cases, understanding the bigger picture of the conflict is crucial. This process entails a comprehensive review of past interactions, related issues, and the complex web of relationships within the team. By uncovering the underlying causes and dynamics, leaders gain valuable insights that can inform their approach to resolving the conflict holistically.

Determining Ways to Achieve the Common Goal

Lastly, you can foster resolution by identifying a shared objective that transcends individual grievances. By aligning all parties' interests toward a common goal, the focus shifts from discord to unity. This shared aim becomes the driving force behind finding innovative ways to reach that goal, ultimately paving the way for reconciliation and harmony within the team.

Effective conflict resolution can lead to positive outcomes in various settings. For example, in 2018, the U.S. Senate faced a significant challenge in agreeing on a spending bill, leading to a potential government shutdown. A group of bipartisan senators convened in Senator Susan Collins's office to negotiate a resolution. To manage the discussions, Collins introduced a unique method: using a Maasai tribal talking stick, which allowed only the person holding it to speak. This approach facilitated orderly and inclusive communication. Ultimately, the group successfully negotiated a deal to reopen the government. This incident highlights the effectiveness of innovative conflict resolution methods in high-stakes scenarios and demonstrates how creative techniques can lead to constructive outcomes in complex negotiations.

THE IMPORTANCE OF ADAPTABILITY IN LEADERSHIP

As a leader in today's rapidly changing business environment, your adaptability transcends being a mere skill—it stands as an essential element of your leadership. The capacity to modify strategies in response to technological advancements, shifts in the market, and evolving consumer preferences is imperative. Your role involves proactive leadership, guiding your team through these transformations.

Adaptability shines as a symbol of resilience and innovation in a business world where change is the only certainty. Recognizing that this flexibility can be cultivated and enhanced is key. Leadership development programs provide critical resources and insights to strengthen your adaptability.

In steering your team, embracing change goes beyond merely keeping up; it involves being a trailblazer. Maintaining adaptability cultivates a culture of agility and ongoing improvement within your team. This strategy not only equips your organization to meet current challenges but also places it in an advantageous position for future opportunities.

Your pivotal role in driving this change, coupled with your enthusiasm and readiness to adapt, is crucial for successful navigation into the future.

Embracing adaptability leads to enhanced decision-making and fosters a culture of innovation. Here's how to do so:

- **Flexibility in strategy:** Adaptability empowers you to be flexible in your strategic approach. When circumstances change, which they often do in a dynamic business world, being adaptable allows you to pivot and adjust your strategies effectively. This flexibility ensures that your decisions remain relevant and effective.
- **Feedback integration:** Viewing feedback as an opportunity for improvement rather than just criticism is a hallmark of an adaptable leader. By integrating constructive feedback into your decision-making process, you open the door to diverse perspectives and insights, which can lead to more informed and comprehensive decisions.
- **Scenario planning:** Adaptability involves considering various scenarios and being prepared to modify your decisions as events unfold. This approach helps in anticipating potential challenges and opportunities, allowing for more proactive and strategic decision-making.
- **Test and learn:** Don't hesitate to experiment with new approaches. Conducting small-scale tests or pilot projects can be an effective way to explore innovative ideas and refine your decision-making process. This "test and learn" approach helps in identifying what works best and fosters a culture of continuous improvement and innovation.

TOOLS AND METHODS FOR MANAGING AND ADAPTING TO CHANGE

It's important to remember that adaptability isn't just a reactive measure; it's a proactive strategy that positions you and your organization for future success. By embracing change, preparing for it, and leading it with a clear vision and effective communication, you foster a resilient and agile culture. Here's an overview of strategies and methods for managing change:

- **Plan carefully:** Develop an extensive, detailed plan that accounts for all aspects of the change. This plan should consider potential impacts on processes, people, and technology, ensuring that every angle is covered.
- **Be as transparent as possible:** Foster an environment of trust by being open about the reasons for the change, its expected outcomes, and how it will affect everyone involved. Transparency helps in building support and buy-in for the change.
- **Tell the truth:** Ensure all communications related to the change are honest and straightforward. Avoid sugarcoating or withholding information to build credibility and trust.
- **Communicate effectively:** Maintain regular and clear communication throughout the change process. This includes not just conveying information but also being open to feedback and questions.
- **Create a roadmap:** Develop a clear, concise roadmap that outlines each step in the change process. This tool serves as a guide for everyone involved, helping them understand their role and the overall direction.
- **Provide training:** Offer comprehensive training programs to equip your team with the skills and knowledge needed to adapt to new systems, processes, or expectations.
- **Invite participation:** Actively encourage involvement from team members at all levels. Soliciting input and ideas can lead to more effective and inclusive change strategies.

- **Acknowledge the time required:** Recognize that implementing change is a gradual process. Setting realistic timelines helps manage expectations and reduces pressure on the team.
- **Monitor and measure:** Regularly assess the progress of the change implementation. Use measurable indicators to track success and identify areas that need adjustment.
- **Demonstrate strong leadership:** Exhibit leadership qualities that inspire and guide your team through the change. Strong leadership involves not just directing but also supporting and empowering your team.
- **Focus on the positives:** Highlight the benefits and opportunities that come with change. This positive focus can motivate and encourage a more receptive attitude toward the change.
- **Embrace change:** Develop and nurture a culture that sees change as a regular and necessary part of growth and improvement. This mindset helps in reducing resistance to change.
- **Prepare for future changes:** Anticipate future trends and challenges. Proactive planning allows for smoother transitions when changes occur.
- **Adopt a flexible mindset:** Encourage a mindset open to new perspectives and ways of working. Flexibility in thinking enables quicker adaptation to new situations.
- **Set new goals:** Align your objectives and goals with the new direction. This step helps in giving a clear focus and purpose post-change.
- **Communicate concerns:** Create channels for open discussion about worries or issues related to the change. Addressing concerns head-on can alleviate anxiety and foster a more supportive environment.
- **Focus on controllable aspects:** Concentrate on elements within your influence. This approach helps in managing change more effectively.

- **Prepare for worst-case scenarios:** Understand potential risks and have contingency plans in place. Being prepared for the worst helps in mitigating risks and reduces the fear of the unknown.
- **Manage stress:** Encourage techniques and practices that help in managing stress. Maintaining a calm and balanced approach is vital during times of change.

Exercises for Developing Adaptability Skills

Engaging in adaptability activities can empower your workforce to excel in the dynamic and evolving work landscape. When your employees possess a high degree of adaptability, they not only communicate effectively with colleagues but also excel in problem-solving and collaborate seamlessly within their teams.

These exercises and activities cater to various learning styles and preferences while fostering adaptability skills. Incorporate a mix of these activities into your training or development programs to help individuals become more adept at navigating change and uncertainty.

- **Diversity poll:** In this activity, team members are asked to respond to polls on a range of topics, from personal preferences to professional opinions. This exercise encourages participants to recognize and value the diversity of thought and experience within their team. It challenges them to consider different viewpoints and adapt their perspectives, enhancing their ability to work in diverse environments.
- **Dream workplace:** Participants articulate their vision of an ideal work environment, encompassing everything from office layout to company culture. This exercise not only fosters creativity but also opens minds to a variety of workplace preferences. Understanding and appreciating these differences helps in adapting to and embracing diverse work cultures.

- **Flying balloons:** A dynamic and engaging activity where participants strive to keep balloons airborne. It demands quick reflexes and adaptation to sudden changes, mimicking the unpredictability of real-world scenarios. This activity teaches the importance of staying alert and responsive in a constantly changing environment.
- **Name choices:** For this activity, participants select new names for themselves and explain their choices. This imaginative exercise promotes creativity and self-expression. It encourages participants to explore new identities and perspectives, enhancing openness to change and fostering adaptability in personal and professional interactions.
- **Puzzled hands:** Teams work together to solve puzzles but with a unique challenge such as using only one hand. This twist introduces unexpected difficulties, forcing teams to think creatively and work collaboratively. It's a practical demonstration of adapting to and overcoming unforeseen challenges.
- **Rescue ship:** In this scenario-based exercise, participants must decide who to save in a hypothetical sinking ship situation. This activity tests decision-making skills and moral reasoning in high-pressure situations. It emphasizes the need for quick thinking and adaptability in critical decision-making processes.
- **Silent concert:** This exercise in non-verbal communication has participants express thoughts and emotions without words. This activity enhances adaptability to different communication styles and underscores the importance of non-verbal cues in effective communication.
- **Transforming words:** This fast-paced word association game requires participants to quickly shift their thoughts and respond to new prompts. This activity sharpens mental agility and fosters an adaptable mindset, which is essential for brainstorming and innovative thinking.

- **Virtual teammate:** Simulating remote teamwork scenarios, this activity prepares participants for the realities of virtual collaboration. Each team member is assigned a specific role, and clear objectives are provided. Teams utilize virtual communication tools and work on the assigned scenario, mirroring the challenges of remote work. Afterward, a debriefing session fosters discussion on communication effectiveness, trust-building, and adaptability, ultimately equipping participants with essential skills for thriving in virtual work environments.
- **Web passage:** In this physical challenge, participants navigate through a web-like structure. This activity symbolizes the journey of overcoming obstacles and adapting strategies to navigate complex situations. It highlights the importance of persistence, flexibility, and problem-solving in a physical and metaphorical web of challenges.

Leadership Scenarios

Let's explore some fictional yet realistic scenarios illustrating successful adaptation in various leadership contexts:

Technology Upgrade in a Financial Firm:

Scenario: You are the CTO of a mid-sized financial firm that has been relying on outdated technology. The firm is struggling to keep up with competitors who are using more advanced systems.

Adaptive challenge: The challenge is not just technical but also cultural, as employees are accustomed to the old systems.

Adaptive leadership approach:

- Conduct focus groups and surveys to understand employee apprehensions and needs.

- Develop a comprehensive change management plan that includes training programs for employees to ease the transition.
- Implement a phased rollout of the new technology, accompanied by regular feedback sessions to address any concerns and make adjustments.
- Lead by example by being the first to adopt and advocate for the new technology.

Outcome: Over time, the firm successfully transitions to the new technology, with employees adapting well to the change. The firm's operational efficiency improves, gaining a competitive edge in the market.

Retail Chain Responds to E-Commerce Growth:

Scenario: You are the CEO of a national retail chain experiencing declining sales due to the rise of e-commerce.

Adaptive challenge: The challenge involves shifting the business model to integrate online shopping while retaining the brick-and-mortar store appeal.

Adaptive leadership approach:

- Collaborate with a team of e-commerce experts to develop an online shopping platform that complements the physical stores.
- Initiate a company-wide training program to equip employees with the skills needed for the digital transition.
- Launch a marketing campaign to promote the new online platform, emphasizing the convenience of multiple shopping options.
- Regularly review customer feedback and sales data to continuously improve the online shopping experience.

Outcome: The retail chain successfully establishes a significant online presence, revitalizing the brand and attracting a broader customer base. The blend of online and in-store shopping experiences leads to a recovery in sales and enhanced customer loyalty.

In each of these scenarios, the leaders identify and address not only the immediate technical challenges but also the underlying adaptive challenges, leading to successful and sustainable change.

CONFLICT RESOLUTION ROLE-PLAYING SCENARIOS

Here are two conflict resolution role-playing scenarios inspired by the provided resources. These scenarios can be used in a group setting to practice different conflict resolution strategies. These role-playing exercises are effective in developing conflict resolution skills, as they provide a safe space to explore and practice different strategies.

Scenario 1: The Project Deadline Dispute

Background: Two team members, Samantha and Richard, are working on a project together. The deadline is approaching, and there's still a lot of work to be done. Samantha wants to ask for an extension, believing that quality should take precedence. Richard disagrees, arguing that meeting deadlines is crucial to maintain credibility with the client.

Roles:

- Samantha: She believes in asking for an extension to improve the project's quality.
- Richard: He insists on meeting the deadline to maintain reliability.
- Moderator/facilitator: They observe the interaction and provide feedback.

Objective: Find a mutually acceptable solution that addresses the concerns of both parties without compromising the project's quality or deadline.

Scenario 2: Office Space Redesign

Background: The office is being redesigned, and there's a disagreement over the layout. Sam prefers an open-plan layout to foster collaboration, while Riley wants individual cubicles for privacy and concentration.

Roles:

- Sam: He advocates for an open-plan office for better collaboration.
- Riley: She wants cubicles for privacy and better focus.
- Moderator/facilitator: They guide the discussion and ensure both parties are heard.

Objective: Develop a compromise that balances the need for collaboration with the need for private workspaces.

How to Conduct These Role-Playing Scenarios:

There can be many ways to conduct these scenarios:

- **Assign roles:** Each participant should be assigned a role (e.g., Alex, Jordan, Sam, Riley, or facilitator).
- **Understand the background:** Participants should familiarize themselves with the scenario's background and their character's viewpoint.
- **Act out the scenario:** Participants engage in a dialogue, staying in character, to resolve the conflict.

- **Facilitator's role:** The facilitator guides the discussion, ensuring each participant has the opportunity to express their views and concerns.
- **Debrief:** After the role-play, discuss what strategies were effective, what could be improved, and how each participant felt during the process.

As we conclude this chapter, let's reflect on the crucial insights we've gained. We delved into the dynamic realms of conflict resolution and adaptability in leadership, underscoring the importance of these skills in today's ever-evolving business landscape. Through practical exercises like conflict resolution role-playing and real-world inspired scenarios, we've equipped you with tools to navigate and manage conflict effectively. We also explored various methods and exercises to foster adaptability—a key trait for modern leaders.

Now, it's your turn to bring these concepts to life. Implement these strategies in your daily interactions and decision-making processes. Reflect on how you manage conflict and embrace change, and consider how you can apply these techniques to become a more effective and adaptable leader. Remember, the real test of these lessons lies in their application in real-world scenarios, be it in your team, organization, or personal life.

Looking ahead, prepare to dive into the emotional depths of leadership in our next chapter. This chapter promises to be an enlightening journey into how understanding and managing emotions can significantly enhance your leadership effectiveness.

So, as we transition from the mechanics of conflict resolution and adaptability to the more nuanced aspects of emotional intelligence, get ready to bridge the gap between intellect and emotion in leadership. This journey will not only enhance your leadership skills but also enrich your personal growth and relationships.

CHAPTER 7
AWARENESS OF EMOTIONS: EMOTIONAL INTELLIGENCE IN LEADERSHIP

"The emotionally intelligent person is skilled in four areas: identifying emotions, using emotions, understanding emotions, and regulating emotions."

JOHN MAYER

Think of the best leader you've ever known. Chances are, their emotional intelligence was as impressive as their strategic thinking. This chapter reveals how honing your emotional intelligence, sometimes referred to as "EI," can be your greatest asset in leadership —transforming the way you connect, empathize, and lead your team.

The essence of this chapter is to highlight the significance of developing key components of EI: self-awareness and empathy. These aren't just buzzwords; they are foundational skills that contribute to superior leadership. You'll learn not only the theoretical underpinnings of EI but also practical ways to enhance these skills. The goal is to equip you with the tools necessary for managing your emotions and understanding those of your team members, leading to improved communication, decision-making, and ultimately, a more harmonious and productive workplace.

As you progress through the chapter, remember that developing emotional intelligence is a journey. It requires patience, practice, and a willingness to be vulnerable and open to feedback. The rewards are immense—not just in enhanced leadership capabilities, but in deeper, more meaningful professional and personal relationships.

THE ROLE OF EMOTIONAL INTELLIGENCE IN LEADERSHIP

Emotional Intelligence is crucial in leadership as it encompasses the ability to understand, manage, and use emotions effectively in both oneself and others. In leadership, EI is a pivotal force that drives inter-personal interactions, decision-making, and problem-solving. It comprises five key components:

1. **Self-awareness:** This component is the foundation of EI. In leadership, self-awareness means being cognizant of your emotions, strengths, weaknesses, and the impact of your

actions on others. A self-aware leader can accurately assess their effectiveness, recognize their emotional triggers, and understand how their mood and emotions influence the team.

2. **Self-regulation:** Leaders who excel in self-regulation can control impulsive feelings and behaviors, manage their emotions in healthy ways, and adapt to changing circumstances. This component involves being trustworthy, displaying integrity, and being comfortable with ambiguity and change.

3. **Internal motivation:** Unlike external factors like money or status, internal motivation in leaders stems from an inner passion to pursue goals with energy and persistence. This intrinsic motivation drives leaders to remain optimistic even in the face of failure, and it fosters a strong commitment to the organization and its objectives.

4. **Empathy:** A leader with high empathy can understand and share the feelings of others. This component is critical for managing a successful team or organization. Empathetic leaders are good at recognizing the emotional needs of their employees, which can lead to better handling of sensitive situations and conflicts.

5. **Social skills:** In leadership, social skills are about managing relationships and building networks. Leaders with strong social skills are excellent communicators and adept at building and maintaining relationships. They are good at managing change and persuading and influencing others, crucial for leading a team or organization effectively.

How EI Impacts Leadership Effectiveness, Team Morale, and Organizational Success

EI significantly impacts leadership effectiveness, team morale, and organizational success. Leaders who lead with emotional intelligence can establish deeper emotional connections with their employees. This emotional resonance fosters trust, a crucial element for effective leadership. The way a leader makes employees feel directly affects their engagement and productivity. Leaders who understand and manage emotions well can create a motivating and positive work environment, leading to higher levels of productivity and better overall performance. Its role in leadership is multifaceted, influencing various aspects of the workplace:

- **Change and uncertainty:** In the face of change and uncertainty, emotions can run high. A leader with high EI can acknowledge these emotions, provide reassurance, and guide the team through the transition. They can turn uncertainty into an opportunity for growth, maintaining team focus and morale.

- **Interactions with colleagues:** Daily interactions with colleagues are laden with emotional undertones. An emotionally intelligent leader can navigate these interactions effectively, ensuring clear communication and fostering a positive working environment. They can mediate disputes, encourage collaboration, and build a supportive team culture.
- **Conflict and relationships:** Conflicts are inevitable in any workplace. Leaders with strong EI are better equipped to manage conflicts by understanding the emotional drivers behind them. They can transform conflicts into constructive discussions, strengthening relationships rather than fracturing them.
- **Effort and burnout:** Recognizing the signs of overwork and burnout is crucial. Leaders with high EI can identify when team members are stretched too thin and take steps to alleviate their burden. By doing so, they help maintain a sustainable work pace, ensuring long-term productivity and well-being.
- **Achievement and failure:** How a leader responds to both success and failure impacts the team's emotional state. Celebrating achievements in a way that uplifts the team and handling failures in a constructive manner that encourages learning and resilience is key. An emotionally intelligent leader ensures that failures are seen as stepping stones to success, fostering a growth mindset within the team.

In today's work environment, where mental health and emotional well-being are increasingly prioritized, leaders who can demonstrate empathy, understanding, and emotional support are more likely to foster a positive and productive workplace. In fact, many industries are taking steps toward encouraging a healthy work environment for their employees. According to a study, 74% of employees express a desire for managers who exhibit a leadership style focused on empathy and a supportive attitude (May, 2023a). This statistic highlights the growing preference for leaders who can understand and relate to their team members' emotional needs. Plus, a notable 70% of respondents in a survey indicated that having the right support available for their mental well-being is important to their working life (Milroy Christy & Aloysius, 2010). This research shows how leaders play a role in providing an environment where employees feel emotionally supported, which is directly linked to their overall well-being and job satisfaction.

DEVELOPING SELF-AWARENESS AND EMPATHY

Self-awareness involves a deep understanding of your emotions, strengths, weaknesses, and behaviors, and how these affect others. It is crucial for leaders as it influences decision-making, communication, and the ability to handle stress. Similarly, empathy involves understanding and sharing the feelings of others. It is essential in the workplace to build trust, improve team collaboration, and enhance employee morale.

- **Keep an open mind:** Being open to new ideas and perspectives is essential in today's diverse workplace. It involves challenging your own beliefs and assumptions, being willing to learn from others, and adapting to new information and changing circumstances. An open-minded leader fosters an inclusive and innovative environment.
- **Be mindful of strengths and weaknesses:** A regular self-assessment of your abilities and areas for improvement allows you to leverage your strengths effectively and work on your weaknesses. This awareness enables you to delegate tasks appropriately and seek development where needed, leading to overall personal and professional growth.
- **Stay focused:** Maintaining clarity on your goals and objectives helps navigate through distractions and prioritize effectively. It involves setting clear targets, developing a plan to achieve them, and regularly reviewing progress. Staying focused ensures consistent movement toward your goals.

- **Set boundaries:** Knowing and communicating your limits is crucial for maintaining work-life balance and preventing burnout. Setting boundaries involves saying no when necessary, managing your time effectively, and ensuring that your personal and professional lives are in harmony.
- **Know your emotional triggers:** Understanding what situations or actions trigger negative emotions in you can help in managing your reactions. This self-knowledge enables you to anticipate and prepare for these triggers, leading to more composed and effective responses.
- **Embrace your intuition:** Trusting your gut feelings in decision-making can be a valuable tool. Your intuition often draws on your past experiences and knowledge, even if you're not consciously aware of it. Listening to your inner voice can provide guidance in complex situations where data may be incomplete.
- **Practice self-discipline:** Developing and maintaining healthy habits and behaviors is key to personal and professional success. Self-discipline involves setting rules for yourself, following through on commitments, and resisting short-term temptations for long-term gains.
- **Consider how actions affect others:** Reflect on how your decisions and actions impact your team and colleagues. This reflection should involve thinking beyond your personal perspective and considering the broader implications of your actions, leading to more empathetic and responsible leadership.
- **Apologize when necessary:** Acknowledging your mistakes and offering sincere apologies when you're wrong is crucial for building trust and respect. It shows humility and accountability, which are important traits in a leader.
- **Ask for feedback:** Actively seeking feedback from peers, superiors, and subordinates can provide valuable insights into how you are perceived and where you can improve.

Constructive feedback is a critical component of personal and professional development.

- **Start noticing your reactions:** Pay close attention to how you react emotionally in various situations, particularly in interactions with others. This awareness can help you understand your emotional patterns and triggers, allowing you to manage your responses more effectively.

- **Learn to pause:** Before reacting to a situation, especially in moments of stress or anger, take a moment to pause. This brief respite gives you time to process your emotions and respond in a more measured, thoughtful way, rather than reacting impulsively.

- **Be kind to yourself, always:** Practice self-compassion by treating yourself with the same kindness and understanding that you would offer to others. This approach helps in developing a positive self-image and reduces the tendency to be overly critical of oneself.

- **Get curious:** Cultivate a genuine interest in understanding the experiences and viewpoints of your team members. This curiosity leads to better communication, stronger relationships, and a deeper appreciation of diverse perspectives.

- **Challenge your assumptions:** Avoid making snap judgments or assumptions about people or situations. Instead, take the time to gather more information and understand the context. This approach helps in making more informed and fair decisions.

- **Learn not to take things personally:** In a professional setting, it's important to distinguish between personal feelings and professional feedback or criticism. Learning not to take things personally helps in maintaining objectivity and focusing on constructive growth.

- **Be accountable:** Acknowledge when you make mistakes and take responsibility for your actions. This accountability is key to building trust and respect in professional relationships. It also sets a positive example for your team.

- **Journal:** Keeping a journal can be a powerful tool for self-reflection. Regularly writing about your daily interactions and emotions helps in gaining deeper insights into your behavioral patterns and emotional responses.
- **Practice meditation and mindfulness:** Meditation and mindfulness practices can greatly enhance your ability to stay present and connected with others. These practices aid in developing a calm and focused mind, improving your capacity for empathy and understanding.
- **Live in integrity:** Ensure that your actions are consistently aligned with your values and principles. Living with integrity fosters trust and respect from others and enhances your sense of self-respect and authenticity.

How Empathy Strengthens Leadership

Empathy plays a crucial role in strengthening leadership. By being empathetic, leaders gain a deeper understanding of their employees, fostering a workplace culture characterized by trust, open communication, and effective problem-solving. Let's explore how empathy enhances leadership:

- **Gaining awareness of employee needs:** Empathetic leaders are attuned to the needs and concerns of their employees. For example, a manager noticing an employee's prolonged distress over work-life balance might offer flexible working hours or additional support, demonstrating an understanding of their situation.
- **Creating an environment of open communication and effective feedback:** Empathy allows leaders to create a safe space where employees feel comfortable sharing their thoughts and concerns. A leader who actively listens and

responds with understanding to feedback can foster a more open and communicative team environment.

- **Understanding and resolving employee problems:** Empathetic leaders can better understand the challenges faced by their team members and assist in finding solutions. For instance, a leader might recognize the root causes of a team's declining performance and address them with targeted training or a restructuring of workloads.
- **Validating employee experiences:** When leaders acknowledge and validate their employees' experiences, it builds trust and loyalty. An example of this validation could be a leader acknowledging the stress caused by a high-stakes project and providing additional resources or support to the team.
- **Establishing relationships and trust:** Empathy helps in building strong, trust-based relationships with team members. Leaders who show genuine concern for their employees' well-being establish deeper connections, which are crucial for team cohesion and loyalty.
- **Increasing collaboration and communication:** An empathetic leader can enhance team collaboration by understanding different viewpoints and fostering effective communication. This process might involve mediating conflicts or encouraging diverse perspectives in team discussions.
- **Driving employee engagement and well-being:** By being attuned to their employees' emotional states, empathetic leaders can take steps to ensure their teams are engaged and healthy, both mentally and physically. These steps could include implementing wellness programs or ensuring workloads are manageable.
- **Inspiring and motivating others:** Empathetic leadership can be highly motivating. For example, a leader who recognizes and appreciates individual contributions can boost morale and inspire the team to strive for excellence.

- **Adapting to change and resolving issues:** In times of change or crisis, an empathetic leader can navigate the team through uncertainty by understanding their fears and providing clear, compassionate guidance.

The concepts of self-awareness and empathy are not just theoretical ideals; they are practical tools that have a profound impact on leadership effectiveness and organizational outcomes. A study showcases how a leader's empathy played a crucial role in driving sustainable practices within an organization. The leader's ability to understand and appreciate the concerns of various stakeholders—including employees, customers, and the community—led to the implementation of environmentally friendly policies and practices. This empathetic leadership approach not only improved the organization's sustainability performance but also enhanced its reputation and stakeholder relationships (Linvill & Onosu, 2023).

Let's look at another example. A CEO of a multinational corporation faced declining employee morale and high turnover rates. Recognizing the issue, the CEO began to hold regular open forums and one-on-one meetings with employees at all levels. Through these interactions, the CEO demonstrated genuine empathy, listening to employees' concerns and experiences. This empathetic approach led to significant changes in company policies, improving work-life balance and workplace culture. The result was a notable increase in employee satisfaction and retention, demonstrating how empathy can directly impact organizational health and success (*A Story of Leadership Growth*, 2022).

PRACTICAL EXERCISES FOR ENHANCING EMOTIONAL INTELLIGENCE

Enhancing emotional intelligence is a continuous process that can be fostered through various practical exercises and daily practices. Here are some suggestions to help build EI skills:

- **Who are you?:** Dedicate time to introspectively consider your identity, values, and core beliefs. Understand how these aspects shape your perception, reactions, and interactions with others. This self-knowledge is crucial for authentic and emotionally intelligent leadership.
- **Monitor your inner voice:** Regularly observe and analyze your internal dialogue. Is it critical or supportive? Being aware of your inner voice and learning to reframe negative self-talk to a more positive and encouraging tone can significantly improve your self-esteem and emotional well-being.
- **Your superpower and kryptonite:** Identify your key strengths (superpowers) and areas of vulnerability (kryptonite). Acknowledging and understanding these areas can help you leverage your skills more effectively and address

your weaknesses, leading to personal and professional growth.

- **Write morning pages:** Start each day by writing down your spontaneous thoughts for a few minutes. This stream-of-consciousness writing can clear mental clutter, enhance self-awareness, and provide clarity on your emotional state.
- **Perception/reality:** Reflect on how you perceive yourself versus how others may perceive you. This comparison can uncover discrepancies in self-awareness and present opportunities for personal development and improved interpersonal relationships.
- **The three whys:** In moments of decision-making or emotional response, ask yourself "why" three times to delve deeper into your underlying motivations and emotional drivers. This technique fosters deeper self-understanding and mindful decision-making.
- **Record your ABCs (Activator, Belief, Consequence):** Document events or situations (Activators) that trigger emotional reactions, explore the Beliefs that fuel these emotions, and consider the Consequences of these emotions on your behavior. This exercise aids in understanding and managing emotional responses more effectively.
- **Your best and worst self:** Reflect on instances when you were at your best and your worst. Analyze the triggers and circumstances of these moments to understand what brings out your optimal performance versus what leads to less desirable outcomes.
- **Write your own obituary:** Engage in this reflective exercise to ponder the legacy you wish to leave behind. It helps align your current actions and decisions with your long-term goals and values.
- **Regularly ask for feedback:** Proactively seek feedback from others to gain an external perspective on your emotional impact and behavior. This feedback can be instrumental in improving your self-awareness and interpersonal skills.

- **Get an accountability partner:** Partner with someone who will hold you accountable for your emotional intelligence development. This person can provide objective feedback and support as you work toward your EI goals.
- **The Johari window:** Utilize this psychological tool to better understand your relationship with yourself and others. It helps in identifying both known and unknown aspects of your personality, thus enhancing self-awareness and interpersonal dynamics.
- **The wheel of life:** Assess various aspects of your life, such as career, relationships, health, and personal growth, to understand where your emotional intelligence might need more focus. This holistic view can help you balance different areas of your life and identify where emotional skills can be improved.
- **Name your emotions:** Practice identifying and labeling your emotions as they occur. This exercise enhances your ability to recognize and understand your emotional states, leading to better emotional regulation and empathy.
- **Reflect on past decisions:** Look back at significant decisions in your life and consider the emotional influences behind them. Reflecting on how emotions played a role in these decisions can provide insights into your decision-making patterns and help you make more balanced choices in the future.

REAL-WORLD LEADERSHIP SCENARIOS

Here are examples from real-world case studies that illustrate the application and benefits of emotional intelligence exercises in leadership:

Emotional Intelligence in Healthcare Leadership

In the healthcare sector, a study from eSoftSkills highlighted the transformation of a hospital unit's leadership. The department head began practicing emotional intelligence exercises, such as reflective journaling and seeking feedback. These exercises led to improved self-awareness and better management of stressful situations. As a result, the leader was able to create a more positive work environment, leading to increased team morale and improved patient care (Team, 2023).

People-First Leadership at FedEx Express

A case study by Six Seconds examined how FedEx Express implemented emotional intelligence training for its leaders. One leader, in particular, focused on developing empathy and self-awareness through exercises like active listening and the Johari window. This shift to a more emotionally intelligent leadership style resulted in enhanced team collaboration, higher employee satisfaction, and improved operational efficiency (Freedman, 2014).

Emotional Intelligence in Business Leadership

RocheMartin's case studies demonstrate how business leaders across various industries have benefited from EI training. For instance, a CEO who practiced mindfulness and emotional journaling was able to better understand his emotional triggers and responses. This improved level of understanding led to more empathetic and effective communication with his team, fostering a culture of trust and open dialogue. The result was a more resilient and agile organization, capable of navigating complex business challenges more effectively (*Perform at Your Peak*, n.d.).

EMOTIONAL INTELLIGENCE SELF-ASSESSMENT

Incorporating an interactive element is an excellent way to engage your readers and provide them with a hands-on tool to assess their emotional intelligence. Below is a self-assessment questionnaire. Be honest in your responses. Use this self-assessment as a starting point for your journey to enhance your emotional intelligence. Use the following scale for each question:

- 1 - Strongly disagree
- 2 - Disagree
- 3 - Neutral
- 4 - Agree
- 5 - Strongly agree

Self-Awareness

1. I can easily identify my own emotions as they arise.
2. I am aware of how my emotions affect my decisions and actions.
3. I regularly reflect on my strengths and weaknesses.
4. I am open to feedback, even when it's critical.

Empathy

1. I can effectively understand and relate to the emotions of others.
2. I actively listen and try to see situations from other people's perspectives.
3. I am skilled at diffusing tense situations by showing empathy.
4. I am comfortable discussing emotions with colleagues or team members.

Self-Management

1. I can regulate my emotions, even in stressful situations.
2. I am adaptable and can adjust to changing circumstances without getting overly emotional.
3. I set clear goals and work steadily toward them, regardless of setbacks.
4. I maintain a positive attitude, even in challenging times.

Relationship Management

1. I can build and maintain positive relationships with colleagues and team members.
2. I am skilled at resolving conflicts and finding common ground.
3. I am a good communicator and can convey my ideas clearly.
4. I actively seek opportunities to collaborate with others.

Scoring:

- Add up your scores for each question.
- The higher your total score, the higher your emotional intelligence.

As we conclude this chapter on the power of emotional intelligence in leadership, let's recap the key takeaways and encourage you to take actionable steps to further develop your emotional intelligence.

Throughout this chapter, we've illuminated the vital role of emotional intelligence in effective leadership. We've explored how self-awareness and empathy are the cornerstones of outstanding leadership, providing a deeper connection with your team and enhancing communication and decision-making. We've also equipped you with practical exercises and strategies to enhance your EI, ensuring that these concepts are not just theoretical but applicable in your leadership journey.

With a deeper understanding of emotional intelligence under our belt, we now turn to skills that every leader needs to master: time management and effective delegation. In the next chapter, "Time Management and Effective Delegation," we will explore how to efficiently manage your most precious resource, time, and how to empower your team through delegation. Get ready to learn how to balance your workload and maximize your team's potential.

Your journey to becoming an emotionally intelligent and impactful leader has just begun, and the next chapter promises to further enrich your leadership toolkit. Stay engaged, stay committed, and watch your leadership skills flourish.

CHAPTER 8

REGULATE TIME AND TASKS: EFFICIENT DELEGATION STRATEGIES

"We accomplish all that we do through delegation - either to time or to other people."

STEPHEN R. COVEY

T ime is the one resource that, once lost, you can never get back. Mastering time management and delegation isn't just about getting more done; it's about getting the right things done. This chapter is your guide to transforming into a leader who not only achieves more but also empowers their team to do the same.

In this pivotal chapter, we will discuss the role of efficient time management and effective delegation—skills that are absolutely vital for anyone in a leadership role. Our journey will be structured around two key pillars: prioritization and delegation, each with its own set of strategies to unravel.

As we progress through this chapter, remember that our goal is not merely to help you accomplish more tasks. Our goal goes beyond task completion. We aim to empower you to lead with purpose, striking a balance between your personal and team obligations. Ultimately, this balance will not only boost your productivity but also enhance your overall well-being. So, fasten your seatbelts as we embark on a journey toward becoming a more efficient and impactful leader.

PRINCIPLES OF TIME MANAGEMENT FOR LEADERS

Time is often referred to as the most valuable resource, and this concept is especially true when considering leadership roles. As leaders, we bear the responsibility of steering our teams toward success, and effective time management is the key that unlocks the doors to achievement. Our time is not just a personal asset; it is a valuable resource that must be wisely allocated to benefit not only ourselves but also our organization and stakeholders.

Consider for a moment the consequences of poor time management. Missed deadlines, projects spiraling out of control, and a constant state of overwhelm hinder our productivity and have a ripple effect on our team members. Their motivation and performance can suffer when they don't receive clear guidance or when deadlines are constantly missed. The stress levels rise, and the harmony within the team begins to waver.

Good time management can lead to a healthy, balanced lifestyle that may manifest in any of the following outcomes:

Reducing Stress

Efficient time management serves as a formidable tool for reducing stress levels. It allows individuals to approach their tasks with a clear and focused mind, devoid of the burdensome weight of impending deadlines or the disarray that can arise from an overwhelming workload. This methodical approach to time allocation not only enhances mental and emotional well-being but also promotes rational decision-making and effective problem-solving—qualities that are paramount for any accomplished leader.

Increasing Energy

The practice of judiciously allocating one's time acts as a reservoir for energy. By preventing the exhaustion that comes from overexertion and ensuring adequate rest, individuals conserve their energy for the most demanding and vital tasks. This energy conservation not only keeps them physically and mentally alert but also contributes to an overall sense of vitality. As leaders, having the energy to tackle challenges head-on and inspire their teams is an invaluable asset that can greatly contribute to success.

Achieving Goals Efficiently

Time management functions as the compass that guides individuals toward their goals. When time is effectively structured, every minute contributes to goal attainment with precision and purpose. This structured approach eliminates feelings of aimlessness or being overwhelmed by a multitude of tasks. Achieving goals efficiently not only fosters a sense of accomplishment but also sets a precedent for team members, motivating them to follow suit.

Prioritizing What's Important

Fundamental to time management is the ability to discern between what is urgent and what is truly essential. Individuals develop the skill to identify and prioritize critical tasks, ensuring that they address high-impact activities first. This capacity to focus on what genuinely matters is a game-changer for leaders. It means they allocate their resources and efforts to projects with the most significant positive impact, fostering personal and organizational triumph.

Accomplishing More in Less Time

Through effective time management strategies, individuals unlock the potential to accomplish more within shorter timeframes. They become highly efficient, seamlessly juggling multiple tasks without succumbing to being overwhelmed. This heightened productivity acts as a force multiplier for leadership effectiveness. It enables leaders to take on additional responsibilities, confront complex challenges adeptly, and consistently meet deadlines. The ability to deliver results in less time becomes a hallmark of their leadership style.

Reducing Procrastination

Procrastination, a common productivity hindrance, can be significantly curtailed through effective time management techniques. Individuals learn to break tasks into manageable segments, set deadlines, and cultivate an environment that minimizes distractions. Consequently, tasks are completed promptly, and the nagging guilt often associated with procrastination dissipates. This newfound sense of discipline and focus not only enhances personal productivity but also sets a precedent for team members, promoting a proactive and results-driven work culture.

Boosting Confidence

As individuals adeptly manage their time and consistently achieve their goals, confidence naturally blossoms. They gain a sense of mastery over their responsibilities, secure in the knowledge that they possess the skills and discipline needed to tackle challenges. This newfound confidence radiates to their teams, instilling a sense of belief in their abilities. Their confidence serves as a source of inspiration, motivating team members to strive for excellence and reinforcing their leadership presence.

Advancing in Your Career

Enhanced time management is not merely a personal advantage but also a powerful catalyst for career advancement. As individuals consistently demonstrate competence and efficiency, they become highly sought-after leaders within their organizations. Their ability to meet deadlines, deliver results, and lead effectively positions them as competent and efficient leaders. This recognition can open doors to new opportunities, promotions, and career growth that may have previously appeared unattainable.

Time Management Techniques and Tools for Leaders

Effective leadership hinges not only on making critical decisions but also on managing time efficiently. In this section, we will introduce a range of time management techniques and tools specially tailored for leaders. These strategies will empower you to make the most of your time, increase productivity, and lead your team with precision and purpose.

- **Prioritize your tasks:** One of the fundamental principles of time management is differentiating between what's important and urgent versus what's not. Leaders should focus their attention on tasks that fall into the "important and urgent" category. These are the tasks that require immediate attention and align with organizational objectives. By prioritizing effectively, you ensure that your time is directed toward high-impact activities.

- **Use tools and apps:** In the digital age, there is a multitude of productivity tools and apps available to help manage your tasks, schedule your day, set reminders, and more. Leveraging these tools can significantly enhance your time management capabilities. Whether it's a task management app, a calendar tool, or project management software, these resources can streamline your workflow and boost efficiency.

- **Set SMART goals:** Setting goals that are Specific, Measurable, Achievable, Relevant, and Time-bound (SMART) is a cornerstone of effective time management. SMART goals provide clear direction and make tasks more manageable. Leaders who set SMART goals ensure that their efforts are aligned with strategic objectives, facilitating progress and success.

- **Time blocking:** Time blocking is a technique where specific blocks of time are allocated to different tasks or types of work throughout the day. This approach minimizes context switching and enhances focus. Leaders who employ time blocking can devote uninterrupted periods to critical tasks, optimizing productivity.

- **Delegate when possible:** Leaders must recognize that not every task requires their direct involvement. Delegating tasks that can be handled by others allows leaders to focus on responsibilities that demand their specific skills and expertise. Effective delegation is a skill that lightens the leadership load while fostering team growth.

- **Avoid multitasking:** Multitasking, often seen as a sign of efficiency, can actually lead to mistakes and decreased productivity. Leaders should resist the urge to juggle multiple tasks simultaneously and instead concentrate on one task at a time until it is completed. This approach ensures a higher level of quality and attention to detail.

- **Create a structured daily routine:** A structured daily routine provides a roadmap for leaders to navigate their day effectively. It eliminates the need to decide continually what to do next, thus saving valuable time. Leaders can craft routines that align with their objectives, ensuring they maximize every moment.

- **Minimize interruptions:** Leaders often face constant interruptions that disrupt their workflow. To counteract these disruptions, it's essential to create an environment where interruptions are minimized. Strategies may include setting specific office hours, utilizing "do not disturb" mode on devices, or setting boundaries with colleagues to preserve focused work time.

- **Take care of your health:** Leaders mustn't overlook the impact of their health on time management. Regular exercise, a healthy diet, and adequate sleep are essential factors that directly influence energy levels and overall productivity. Prioritizing health ensures leaders can perform at their best.

- **Regularly review and reflect on your work:** At the end of each week, taking time to review accomplishments and identify challenges is a valuable time management practice. It allows leaders to refine their strategies, adapt to changing circumstances, and continually improve their effectiveness.

There are some other tips you can use, such as the following examples:

- Instead of an overwhelming list, keep your to-do list short and focused. Begin by separating the wheat from the chaff. Identify the most crucial tasks that align with your goals and contribute significantly to your objectives. This approach ensures you're not just busy, but productive, concentrating on what truly matters.
- Mindless email checking can consume a significant portion of your day. Instead, set designated times to check and respond to emails. By refraining from robo-checking, you regain control over your schedule and prevent constant interruptions. This strategy allows you to allocate uninterrupted periods for focused work.
- Repetitive emails, such as responses to common queries or requests, can be time-consuming. Consider creating email templates or canned responses for frequently asked questions. This time-saving tactic streamlines your email communication and ensures consistency in your replies.
- A cluttered inbox can be a productivity killer. Implement an email management system that categorizes and prioritizes important messages. Utilize labels, folders, or filters to keep your inbox organized and ensure that crucial emails are readily accessible.
- Your calendar is a potent ally in time management. Schedule your day meticulously, blocking off time for specific tasks and meetings. Ensure that your calendar reflects your priorities and goals. By adhering to your calendar diligently, you optimize your time allocation and reduce the likelihood of missing critical deadlines or appointments.

- Meetings can be time-consuming if they lack clarity and purpose. Kick-off meetings by asking clarifying questions to establish the meeting's objectives, agenda, and desired outcomes. This upfront clarification ensures that meetings stay focused, productive, and on schedule.
- In an effort to allow for thorough discussions, meetings are often scheduled for extended durations. However, setting shorter meeting times can foster efficiency. It encourages participants to stay focused and on-topic, resulting in more concise and effective meetings.
- Scheduling meetings back-to-back can be a strategic move. It minimizes gaps in your schedule, ensuring that pockets of time are not wasted between meetings. This approach compels you to adhere to meeting timelines and encourages promptness.

Examples of How Time Management Leads to Better Leadership Outcomes

Effective time management is crucial for successful leadership. Here are real-life examples illustrating how mastering time management can lead to better leadership outcomes:

Rob Rawson's High Priority Approach

Rob Rawson, the CEO of TimeManagement.com, adopts a strategic approach to his workday by focusing on his most critical tasks right at the start of his day. This tactic ensures that he tackles these high-priority items without the interference of less important activities like checking emails or getting caught up in minor tasks. Moreover, Rawson finds it beneficial to break down larger goals into manageable segments. This method simplifies the progression toward these objectives, making them more attainable and less daunting. By segmenting his goals, Rawson can make steady, tangible progress in achieving his overarching ambitions (Square, 2021).

Julia Kelly's Meeting Agenda

Julia Kelly, the managing partner at Rigits, shares her effective strategy for managing time, particularly in the context of leadership responsibilities. Recognizing the challenges that come with a leader's busy schedule and the pressure of making responsible decisions, she implements a system of individual meetings with her team members.

In her approach, Kelly schedules one-on-one meetings with those who report to her, allowing for focused and direct interaction. To maintain her engagement and efficiency, after every five meetings, she takes a brief break. This period of reflection is a key aspect of her strategy. It provides her with the opportunity to assess the meetings, reset goals, and prepare for the next set of interactions.

This method not only helps her stay fully engaged during each session but also ensures that no team member is overlooked. The reflection time allows her to evaluate and adjust her approach as needed. Importantly, this approach also helps in minimizing the risk of burnout or frustration, both for herself and her team members. The direct interaction afforded to team members through these individual meetings is a crucial element in maintaining a healthy and productive work environment (Featured, 2023).

Rosie Golden's Pomodoro Technique Utilization

Rosie Gladden, the Marketing Director at ImageX, shares her insights on utilizing the Pomodoro Technique for effective time management, especially in her role as a leader and people manager. She highlights that in her busy schedule, filled with calls and meetings, it's crucial to make the most of the short blocks of time available to her.

Gladden has experimented with various methods such as time blocking and scheduling specific times for checking emails. However, she found Francesco Cirillo's Pomodoro Technique to be the most effective in maximizing her day-to-day productivity. This technique involves working in short, focused bursts on a specific task, followed by taking short breaks. These breaks might include activities like making coffee or switching contexts, before diving into the next focused work session.

She also mentions using a productivity planner to organize her tasks but emphasizes the importance of flexibility. Recognizing that her work in a fast-paced organization requires adaptability, she allows for changes in her schedule without frustration if things don't go as initially planned (Featured, 2023).

DELEGATING EFFECTIVELY

Delegation in leadership is a critical skill for effective team management and organizational growth. It involves assigning tasks or responsibilities to others, typically team members or subordinates. When executed properly, delegation benefits both leaders and their teams in several ways:

- **Leadership and workload management:** Delegation allows senior leaders to prioritize their workload more effectively. By distributing tasks, leaders can focus on high-level strategic planning and other responsibilities that only they can perform. This approach helps maintain a balanced workload and prevents burnout.
- **Trust and teamwork:** Effective delegation increases trust within a team. It shows that leaders have confidence in their team members' abilities to handle responsibilities. This trust fosters a stronger team dynamic, where members feel valued and empowered.

- **Ownership and accountability:** When tasks are delegated, employees are given a sense of ownership over their work. They become more accountable for outcomes, which can lead to higher levels of engagement and a deeper sense of commitment to the project and the organization.
- **Skill development:** Delegation is also an opportunity for employee development. When leaders assign challenging tasks, team members can build and enhance their skills, which contributes to their personal growth and the overall talent pool within the organization.
- **Training and promotion:** A study published in Harvard Business Review highlights a significant issue in organizational leadership development. It reveals that while many companies offer leadership development programs, they often attract little interest from employees. This lack of engagement is partly because employees may find these programs too challenging or struggle to commit time to them. The study emphasizes the importance of equipping employees with the necessary skills, including effective delegation, before promoting them to leadership roles. It suggests that internal promotions to leadership positions can be more effective than external hires, as existing employees already understand the company's operations (Robinson, 2018).
- **Under-delegation issues:** Many leaders tend to under-delegate, either due to a lack of trust in their team's abilities or a desire to maintain control. This approach can lead to inefficiencies and missed opportunities for team development.

By understanding and implementing effective delegation strategies, leaders can improve not just their own productivity and stress levels but also contribute to a more capable, motivated, and high-performing team.

Strategies for Delegating Tasks Appropriately

When delegating tasks, it's important to consider your team members' skills and career goals. There are many strategies you can implement:

- **Prioritize trust and transparency:** Build a foundation of trust by being open about why certain tasks are being delegated. Clarify what you expect from the team in terms of results, ensuring they understand the significance of their roles in the broader objectives.
- **Identify tasks to delegate:** Assess your workload and identify tasks that can be delegated. Focus on delegating tasks that match your team members' current skills and areas where they wish to grow, enhancing their development and engagement.
- **Offer guidance without interfering:** Provide clear instructions and necessary resources to your team. While offering guidance is crucial, it's equally important to step back and allow team members to approach the task in their own way, fostering a sense of autonomy.
- **Invest in training:** Ensure your team has the training and resources they need to succeed in the tasks you delegate. This approach might involve formal training sessions, workshops, or one-on-one mentoring.
- **Understand each team member's strengths:** Tailor your delegation strategy to the individual strengths and weaknesses of your team members. This personalized approach can lead to more effective and efficient task completion.
- **Clarify priorities:** Clearly communicate the priority level of each task to help team members manage their time and focus effectively.
- **Provide context and guidance:** Explain how each task fits into the larger picture. This helps team members understand the importance of their work and stay motivated.

- **Prioritize communication and feedback:** Keep the lines of communication open. Regular check-ins and feedback help ensure tasks are on track and provide opportunities for course correction if needed.
- **Focus on results:** Encourage your team to focus on the end goals of their tasks. This results-oriented approach can inspire innovative problem-solving and efficiency.
- **Trust but verify:** Empower your team with autonomy but also implement a system of periodic check-ins to monitor progress and offer support.
- **Give credit once work is completed:** Recognize and appreciate the efforts and achievements of your team. This recognition not only boosts morale but also encourages future engagement and productivity.

BALANCING PERSONAL AND TEAM RESPONSIBILITIES

Balancing personal and professional responsibilities is a significant challenge for leaders, often compounded by several factors:

- **Long working hours:** Extended work hours often stem from job demands or a perceived necessity to meet workplace expectations. This relentless schedule can significantly impinge on personal time, making it challenging for individuals to engage in activities like family bonding, exercise, or hobbies. Such an imbalance can adversely affect personal well-being and relationships.
- **Demanding jobs:** Roles that are inherently high-pressure, with intense workloads and stress, create a situation where individuals find it hard to mentally disconnect from work. This continuous engagement with work, even during supposed downtime, can be a pathway to exhaustion and burnout.

- **Family responsibilities:** Balancing work with family duties, such as parenting or caregiving, demands substantial time and emotional commitment. This dual demand can lead to conflicts between professional obligations and family needs, often leaving little time for self-care or relaxation.
- **Intrusive technology:** The pervasive nature of technology in the form of emails, texts, and social media notifications keeps individuals tethered to their work, blurring the boundaries between professional and personal life. This constant connectivity can make it difficult to truly "switch off" and enjoy personal time.
- **High personal expectations:** The self-imposed pressure to excel in both personal and professional realms can create an internal conflict, leading to stress and guilt, especially when individuals feel they are falling short of their own expectations.
- **Lack of support:** Without understanding and support from employers, families, or friends, achieving a work-life balance becomes more challenging. Insufficient workplace flexibility or a lack of empathy from loved ones regarding work-related stress can exacerbate the difficulty in maintaining this balance.

TIPS AND METHODS FOR MAINTAINING THIS BALANCE

To maintain a healthy work-life balance without compromising team performance or personal well-being, consider incorporating these strategies along with insights from a Business News Daily article (Sanfilippo, 2023):

- Organize your schedule to manage tasks effectively. Prioritize tasks and allocate sufficient time for work and personal activities.
- Understand and utilize your peak productivity times. Align challenging tasks with times when you're most alert.

- Allocate specific time slots for different types of work to increase focus and efficiency.
- Establish a definite end to your workday to create a clear boundary between work and personal time.
- Leverage apps or settings that limit work-related notifications after hours to help you disconnect.
- Step away from work for lunch, either alone or with colleagues, to recharge.
- Regularly schedule vacations or days off to rest and rejuvenate.
- Engage in mindfulness or relaxation techniques to reduce stress and enhance well-being.
- Engage in hobbies or activities outside of work that bring you joy and fulfillment.
- If work consistently encroaches on your personal life, consider discussing workload adjustments or exploring different roles.
- Openly discuss work-life balance needs and expectations with your manager.
- Work with a coach or therapist for personalized strategies to manage stress and balance responsibilities.

LEADERS WHO HAVE SUCCESSFULLY MANAGED THIS BALANCE

Achieving a balance between work and personal life is often seen as the ultimate goal for working professionals. While it requires effort and planning, many across various industries have found it to be entirely feasible. Successfully balancing these aspects often involves a mix of strategy, compromise, and mindful organization. Those who have mastered this balance emphasize its value, suggesting that the benefits of a harmonious work-life integration significantly enhance both professional success and personal fulfillment.

Sheryl Sandberg, Facebook's COO, exemplifies work-life balance by leaving her office at 5:30 p.m. daily. This routine, established during her tenure at Google, allows her to have dinner with her children by 6:00 p.m. Her approach challenges the notion that success necessitates long hours and weekend work. Furthermore, after her husband's passing in 2015, Sandberg's use of Facebook's bereavement leave, which offers up to 20 days off, highlights the company's supportive policies for employees during difficult times.

It recounts the story of Dustin, an employee at Amazon, who faced challenges in balancing his professional commitments with his personal life. Despite his dedication and enthusiasm, Dustin struggled to establish boundaries, which ultimately led him to leave the company. This narrative underscores the critical need for clear communication with managers, prioritization of tasks, and the importance of setting limits to prevent burnout.

Brian Dyson, the former Vice Chairman and COO of Coca-Cola uses a metaphor of juggling five balls to describe life's priorities. He likens work to a rubber ball and the other aspects of life—family, health, friends, and spirit—to glass balls. The essence of his message is that work, unlike the other areas, can rebound if dropped, symbolizing the potential to recover from professional setbacks. However, the other aspects are more fragile and can suffer lasting damage if neglected. This analogy serves as a reminder of the importance of balancing work with other critical life areas, as the consequences of neglecting them can be irreversible.

PERSONAL VERSUS PROFESSIONAL RESPONSIBILITIES CHART

Below is a table that can help you visualize your current state of balance, set goals, and develop actionable strategies to achieve a healthier equilibrium between your personal and professional lives. It serves as a valuable tool for self-assessment and improvement in managing these critical aspects of your life.

Aspect	Personal responsibilities	Professional responsibilities
Time allocation		
Daily routine		
Weekly commitments		
Monthly priorities		
Energy allocation		
Physical energy		
Emotional well-being		
Prioritization		
Top personal priorities		
Top professional priorities		
Goals and objectives		
Personal goals		
Professional goals		
Strategies for balance		
Time management		
Boundary setting		
Support system		
Challenges		
Personal challenges		
Professional challenges		
Strategies for overcoming challenges		
Personal strategies		
Professional strategies		

In this chapter, we've explored essential skills for leadership: time management and effective delegation. We've learned the value of mastering these skills, from reducing stress to achieving goals efficiently. Now, it's time to put these ideas into action. Implement these strategies in your daily life to become a more effective leader.

As we close this chapter on time management and effective delegation, we also conclude our journey through the essential skills of leadership. In the conclusion, we will recap the key lessons from each chapter, tying together the threads of communication, team building, decision-making, and more into a cohesive tapestry of leadership excellence. Get ready to reflect on your journey and envision the path forward as a more effective, empathetic, and successful leader.

CONCLUSION

As we reach the final pages of this book, it's time to distill the wealth of knowledge we've explored into a concise and impactful conclusion. Our journey through the essential skills of leadership has been both enlightening and transformative. Now, let's summarize the core message, reflect on key takeaways, share a success story, and issue a call to action.

At its heart, this book has been a testament to the idea that leadership is a multifaceted journey. It's not merely about occupying a position of authority; it's about inspiring, guiding, and bringing out the best in yourself and those you lead. Effective leadership hinges on mastering a set of fundamental skills, and these skills are the pillars on which successful leadership is built.

Throughout these chapters, we've uncovered a treasure trove of leadership insights. Let's distill them into a few key takeaways:

- Listening actively and communicating effectively lay the foundation for strong leadership. By fostering open and honest dialogue, leaders create an environment where ideas flow freely, collaboration thrives, and trust flourishes.

- A leader is only as strong as their team. Empowerment is the secret sauce that transforms a group of individuals into a high-performing, synergistic unit. When individuals feel valued, respected, and entrusted with responsibilities, they excel.
- Leadership is about navigating uncharted waters, and strategic decision-making is your compass. By analyzing situations, weighing options, and making informed decisions, leaders chart a course toward success.
- Trust is the glue that holds teams together. Building trust through authenticity and integrity is a leader's greatest asset. Strong relationships, both within and beyond your team, are the bridges that facilitate cooperation and collaboration.
- Leaders are catalysts for motivation. Inspiring your team through shared goals, recognizing achievements, and fostering a culture of continuous improvement drives excellence.
- Conflict is a natural part of any dynamic group. Effective leaders embrace conflict as an opportunity for growth. Adaptive conflict management strategies transform discord into constructive dialogue.
- Understanding and regulating emotions is an essential leadership skill. Emotional intelligence fosters empathy, enhances relationships, and enables leaders to connect on a profound level with their teams.
- Time is the most valuable resource, and leaders must harness it wisely. Efficient delegation, prioritization, and the judicious use of time-management techniques free leaders to focus on what truly matters.

Let's consider the inspiring story of Alex, a mid-level manager in a tech company. When Alex embarked on a journey to become a more effective leader, they encountered numerous challenges. Their team struggled with communication issues, morale was low, and deadlines were often missed.

Determined to make a change, Alex implemented the principles discussed in this book. They actively listened to their team's concerns, encouraged open discussions, and empowered team members to take ownership of their work. Alex made strategic decisions that aligned with the company's goals and values, and they built trust by being transparent and consistent in their actions.

Motivation flourished as Alex recognized and celebrated team achievements. Conflict was no longer feared but embraced as an opportunity for growth, and emotional intelligence became a guiding compass in dealing with team dynamics.

Efficient time management ensured that Alex had the bandwidth to lead effectively and provide mentorship to team members. Over time, Alex's team transformed—morale soared, productivity increased, and the company achieved remarkable success.

As we conclude this book, remember that the insights and skills you've gained are vital tools for your leadership development. The LEAD STAR framework is designed to be your guide in this ongoing process. Let's recap that framework:

- **Listen and communicate:** Enhance your skills in engaging in meaningful conversations and active listening.
- **Empower teams:** Foster a culture of collaboration and unity within your team.
- **Analyze and decide:** Strengthen your strategic thinking and decision-making abilities.
- **Develop relationships:** Build and maintain networks based on trust and mutual cooperation.
- **Stimulate motivation:** Inspire and energize your team, driving them toward excellence.
- **Tackle conflicts:** Effectively manage and resolve disputes with understanding and agility.
- **Awareness of emotions:** Cultivate emotional intelligence to deepen interpersonal connections.

- **Regulate time and tasks:** Master the art of efficient delegation and time management.

Take the first step by applying the principles you've learned. Identify specific areas in your leadership role where these insights can make a real difference and commit to action. Whether it's through better communication, strategic decision-making, or enhancing team motivation, use these skills to elevate your leadership effectiveness.

Your feedback is invaluable. If you found this book helpful in your leadership journey, we kindly ask you to leave a review. Your insights can inspire others and help them embark on their own path to leadership excellence.

As you continue on your leadership path, may you be guided by the principles of communication, empowerment, strategy, trust, motivation, conflict management, emotional intelligence, and time management. These are the keys to unlocking your leadership potential and making a lasting impact in your sphere of influence.

GLOSSARY

- **Active listening:** A communication technique that involves fully concentrating, understanding, responding, and remembering what is being said.
- **Change agent network:** A group of individuals within an organization trained and empowered to facilitate change initiatives and drive organizational transformation.
- **Cross-functional teams:** Teams composed of members from different departments or areas of expertise, working together toward a common goal.
- **Cultural competency:** The ability to understand, communicate with, and effectively interact with people across different cultures.
- **Delegation:** The act of assigning tasks and responsibilities to subordinates or team members.
- **Emotional intelligence:** The ability to understand, use, and manage your own emotions in positive ways to relieve stress, communicate effectively, empathize with others, and overcome challenges.
- **Emotional resonance:** A leader's ability to create a connection with team members on an emotional level, fostering a sense of belonging and understanding.
- **Expectancy theory:** A theory suggesting that individuals are motivated when they believe their efforts will lead to desired outcomes.
- **Johari window:** A technique used to help people better understand their relationship with themselves and others,

involving a four-quadrant model with aspects known and unknown to oneself and others.

- **LEAD STAR framework:** A leadership model encompassing key skills for effective management: listening and communicating, empowering teams, analyzing and deciding, developing relationships, stimulating motivation, tackling conflicts, awareness of emotions, and regulating time and tasks.
- **Non-monetary incentives:** Rewards or motivators that are not financial in nature, such as recognition or professional development opportunities.
- **Operational efficiency:** The capability of an enterprise to deliver products or services to its customers in the most cost-effective manner while ensuring the high quality of its products, services, and support.
- **Pomodoro technique:** A time management method that involves working in focused intervals (traditionally 25 minutes), followed by short breaks (traditionally 5 minutes).
- **Power dynamics:** How power works in a workplace—who has it, how they use it, and how it affects people.
- **S-CONNECT framework:** A set of tips to help you connect with people better, like paying attention, showing you care, and listening well.
- **SMART goals:** Specific, Measurable, Attainable, Relevant, Time-bound objectives set by a team or individual.
- **Synergy:** The concept that the collective output and performance of a team are greater than the sum of individual efforts.
- **Team cohesion:** The degree to which team members are able to work alongside one another and are motivated to stay in the group.
- **Team dynamics:** The behavioral relationships and interactions among team members in a group.

- **Time blocking:** A time management method where distinct blocks of time are allocated for specific tasks, minimizing context switching and maximizing focus.
- **Visual mapping techniques:** Tools, such as cause and effect diagrams, that are used to visually organize and analyze the factors contributing to a specific situation or problem.

ABOUT THE PUBLISHER

ELSE Publishing (Effective Leadership Skills for Everyone) is owned by William Edwin Carter.

Edwin decided to publish about leadership skills while he lead a global team of over 300 people while working for The Coca-Cola Company. He noticed the transformational power that good leaders have in an organization. Those that "got it" and did leadership right had strong teams, eager to make change, eager to say "yes", but most importantly were eager to invest in each other. This became a focus and intentional in how to engage, empower, and develop those that managed the best assets of the company.

Edwin had a broad career in agriculture, commodity risk management, data analytics, and supply chain. He currently works with companies on interim roles and advisory positions. He is a two-time graduate of The University of Kentucky with a B.S. and M.S. in Agricultural Economics. Edwin and his wife of near 40 years live in Kennesaw, GA. They have two grown sons.

REFERENCES

admin. (2019, September 5). *12 tips on how to foster teamwork in the workplace.* Elevate Corporate Training. https://www.elevatecorporatetraining.com.au/2019/09/06/12-tips-for-fostering-teamwork-in-the-workplace/

Agius, A. (2023, January 9). *12 crucial strategies for promoting team collaboration.* Hubspot. https://blog.hubspot.com/service/team-collaboration

Alexander, M. (2021, September 3). *5 ways diversity and inclusion help teams perform better.* CIO. https://www.cio.com/article/189194/5-ways-diversity-and-inclusion-help-teams-perform-better.html

Bariso, J. (2018, September 10). *Google spent years studying great teams. These 5 qualities contributed the most to its success.* Inc. https://www.inc.com/justin-bariso/google-spent-years-studying-great-teams-these-5-qualities-contributed-most-to-their-success.html

Blank, A. (2022, April 5). *5 tips to help you engage A diverse audience.* Forbes. https://www.forbes.com/sites/averyblank/2022/04/05/5-tips-to-help-you-engage-a-diverse-audience/?sh=2caa3098233a

Bojic, A. (2022, July 7). *Best communication styles for effective leaders.* Pumble Blog. https://pumble.com/blog/communication-styles-for-leaders/

Boogaard, K. (2023, July 27). *6 activities and templates to unite your cross-functional team.* MiroBlog. https://miro.com/blog/6-activities-templates-unite-cross-functional-team/

Britton, G. (2023, February 21). *12 communication-based team building activities to improve relationships.* Poppulo. https://www.poppulo.com/blog/12-communication-based-team-building-activities-to-improve-relationships

Brownlee, D. (2019, October 20). *5 reasons why trust matters on teams.* Forbes. https://www.forbes.com/sites/danabrownlee/2019/10/20/5-reasons-why-trust-matters-on-teams/?sh=2406748c2d60

Candelario, M. (2022, May 16). *20 Team building activities for work that employees will actually love.* Preply. https://preply.com/en/blog/b2b-team-building-activities-for-work/

Chang, L. (2021, January 14). *Communication breakdown in the workplace: 3 causes and solutions.* Life Intelligence. https://www.lifeintelligence.io/blog/communication-breakdown-in-the-workplace

Cleary, A. (2022, April 6). *5 internal communication case studies and best practices to follow.* ContactMonkey. https://www.contactmonkey.com/blog/internal-communication-case-study

Communication styles: A self-assessment exercise. (n.d.). OGE Faculty Mentoring. https://ogefacultymentoring.web.unc.edu/wp-content/uploads/sites/11490/2016/09/Communication-Styles-assessment-ESAI.pdf

Covey, S. (n.d.). *Stephen Covey quotes.* A-Z Quotes. https://www.azquotes.com/author/3347-Stephen_Covey

Deering, S. (2019, January 4). *Top 7 qualities of a successful team.* Undercover Recruiter. https://theundercoverrecruiter.com/qualities-successful-work-team/

Dhamagadda, T. (2023, May 5). *How to resolve communication breakdown in the workplace?* HubEngage. https://www.hubengage.com/employee-communications/how-to-resolve-communication-breakdown-in-the-workplace/

Diverse businesses outperform their peers by up to 36% - can you afford not to tackle diversity in 2021? (2021). Invigorate. https://www.invigorateplatform.com/insight/diverse-businesses-outperform-their-peers-by-up-to-36-can-you-afford-not-to-tackle-diversity-in-2021/

Does effective communication matter in the workplace? (2023, November 27). HCL Tech. https://www.hcltech.com/knowledge-library/does-effective-communication-matter-in-workplace

Duhigg, C. (2016, February 25). What Google learned from its quest to build the perfect team. *The New York Times.* https://www.nytimes.com/2016/02/28/magazine/what-google-learned-from-its-quest-to-build-the-perfect-team.html

Duncan, C. (2021, December 14). *8 common workplace communication mistakes.* Desk Alerts. https://www.alert-software.com/blog/8-common-workplace-communication-mistakes

Effective business communication case study report. (n.d.). Total Assignment Help. https://www.totalassignmenthelp.com/free-sample/effective-business-communication-case-study

Eisler, M. (2023, April 18). *8 common communication mistakes leaders make.* Wide Lens Leadership. https://widelensleadership.com/8-communication-mistakes-leaders-make/

Events, B. C. (2020, January 8). *Team building objectives.* Best Corporate Events. https://bestcorporateevents.com/team-building-objectives

Fabor, P. (2022, May 26). *6 Examples of team building goals and objectives.* Surf Office. https://www.surfoffice.com/blog/teambuilding-goals-objectives

Farrell, M. (2023, January 6). *Data and intuition: Good decisions need both.* Harvard Business Publishing. https://www.harvardbusiness.org/data-and-intuition-good-decisions-need-both/

Featured. (2023, July 23). *11 leaders weigh in on their top time management techniques.* Fast Company. https://www.fastcompany.com/90925779/top-time-management-techniques

15 team building activities for large groups. (n.d.). Teamland. https://www.teamland.com/post/team-building-activities-for-large-groups

Fostering teamwork and collaboration through 4 stages of group development. (2021, November 1). Knowledge Hub. https://pumble.com/learn/collaboration/fostering-teamwork-and-collaboration/

Freedman, J. (2014, January 15). *Case study: Emotional intelligence improves leadership at fedex.* Six Seconds. https://www.6seconds.org/2014/01/14/case-study-emotional-intelligence-people-first-leadership-fedex-express/

Gallo, C. (2022, November 23). *How great leaders communicate.* Harvard Business Review. https://hbr.org/2022/11/how-great-leaders-communicate

Garfinkle, J. (2019). *7 steps to clear & effective communication.* Garfinkle Executive Coaching. https://garfinkleexecutivecoaching.com/articles/improve-your-communi cation-skills/seven-steps-to-clear-and-effective-communication

Gattig, N. (2021, April 7). *Effective strategies to improve your communication skills.* BetterUp. https://www.betterup.com/blog/effective-strategies-to-improve-your-communication-skills

Haynie, S. (2023, June 5). *How personality type affects team performance and job satisfaction.* Forbes. https://www.forbes.com/sites/forbescoachescouncil/2023/07/05/how-personality-type-affects-team-performance-and-job-satisfaction/?sh=76e69e9a7805

Herrity, J. (2023, February 4). *How to exhibit leadership communication skills.* Indeed Career Guide. https://www.indeed.com/career-advice/career-development/leader ship-communication-skills

Holmes, S. (2020, March 10). *Five tips for communicating with clarity as A leader.* Forbes. https://www.forbes.com/sites/forbescommunicationscouncil/2020/03/10/five-tips-for-communicating-with-clarity-as-a-leader/?sh=4f98b68156ca

How can you tailor your team building program for maximum effectiveness? (n.d.). LinkedIn. https://www.linkedin.com/advice/1/how-can-you-tailor-your-team-build ing-program-ivrdc?utm_campaign=collaborative_articles_all_en&utm_source=rss

How do team roles impact team dynamics? (n.d.). LinkedIn. https://www.linkedin.com/ advice/3/how-do-team-roles-impact-dynamics-skills-teamwork

How to effectively engage with different personality types in the workplace. (n.d.). Superfriend. https://www.superfriend.com.au/blog/article/how-to-effectively-engage-with-different-personality-types-in-the-workplace

The importance of trust in Teams. (2015, January 5). Crowe Associates Ltd. https://www.crowe-associates.co.uk/teams-and-groups/the-importance-of-trust-in-teams/

Indeed Editorial Team. (2023, February 28). *How to achieve teamwork success.* Indeed Career Guide. https://www.indeed.com/career-advice/career-development/team work-success

Kawarsky, S. (2023, June 8). *How leadership skills enhance equality, diversity and inclusion.* The Soft Skills Group. https://www.tssg.ca/leadership-skills-for-developing-equality-diversity-and-inclusion-in-the-workplace/

Kinsey, A. (2019, January 31). *The effects of poor communication in business.* Chron. https://smallbusiness.chron.com/effects-poor-communication-business-345.html

Kirkman Baharom, G., Gaskin Stoverink, T., & Sanyal Kalogiannidis, O. (2022). Effect of team building on employee productivity; A case study of eastpharma company in turkey. *Journal of Human Resource &Leadership, 6*(4), 11–20. https://doi.org/10.53819/81018102t50109

Kulakov, M. (2021, January 25). *Team dynamics 101 — simple steps to your team's success.* Everhour Blog. https://everhour.com/blog/team-dynamics/

Lacinai, A. (2022, May 26). *Clarity in your communication is vital.* Antoni Lacinai. https://antonilacinai.com/news/clarity-in-your-communication-is-vital/

Laker, B., & Pereira, V. (2022, May 31). *4 triggers cause the majority of team conflicts.*

Harvard Business Review. https://hbr.org/2022/05/conflict-is-not-always-bad-but-you-should-know-how-to-manage-it

Linvill, J. S., & Onosu, G. O. (2023). Stories of leadership: Leading with empathy through the COVID-19 pandemic. *Sustainability, 15*(9), 7708. https://doi.org/10.3390/su15097708

May, E. (2023a, April 18). *The statistics on emotional intelligence in the workplace.* Niagara Institute. https://www.niagarainstitute.com/blog/emotional-intelligence-statistics

May, E. (2023b, September 7). *The importance of good professional relationships at work.* Niagara Institute. https://www.niagarainstitute.com/blog/professional-relationships

McDougall, S. (2024, January 17). *5 inspirational stories of people who defeated their debt.* Scotland Debt Solutions. https://www.scotlanddebt.co.uk/articles/personal-debt/5-inspirational-stories-of-people-who-defeated-their-debt

McEwan, D., Ruissen, G. R., Eys, M. A., Zumbo, B. D., & Beauchamp, M. R. (2017). The effectiveness of teamwork training on teamwork behaviors and team performance: A systematic review and meta-analysis of controlled interventions. *PLOS ONE, 12*(1), e0169604. https://doi.org/10.1371/journal.pone.0169604

MICM Consultancy Limited. (2023, October 6). *Techniques for clear and impactful business communication.* LinkedIn. https://www.linkedin.com/pulse/techniques-clear-impactful-business-communication-micmconsultancy/

Milroy Christy , S., & Aloysius, M. (2010, October). The role of emotional intelligence in leadership effectiveness. *Research Gate.* Jaffna University Research Conference. https://www.researchgate.net/publication/224872912_The_Role_of_Emotional_Intelligence_in_Leadership_Effectiveness

Mind Tools Content Team. (n.d.). *10 common communication mistakes.* MindTools. https://www.mindtools.com/ar0qk6t/10-common-communication-mistakes

Moore, M. G. (2023, January 13). *How transparent should you be with your team?* Harvard Business Review. https://hbr.org/2023/01/how-transparent-should-you-be-with-your-team

Murphy, M. (2017). *Quiz: What's your communication style?* Leadership IQ. https://www.leadershipiq.com/blogs/leadershipiq/39841409-quiz-whats-your-communication-style

O'Shea , B., & Barroso , A. (2023, November 21). *What is the average credit score?* NerdWallet. https://www.nerdwallet.com/article/finance/what-is-the-average-credit-score

Pandey, N. (2022, June 6). *Communication skills for effective leadership.* Emeritus. https://emeritus.org/in/learn/why-are-communication-skills-necessary-for-good-leadership/

Pappas, S. (2021, October 1). *What keeps employees motivated.* APA. https://www.apa.org/monitor/2021/10/feature-workers-motivation

Penn LPS. (2023, August 9). *Why communication is essential to effective leadership.* Penn LPS. https://lpsonline.sas.upenn.edu/features/why-communication-essential-effective-leadership

Perform at your peak. (n.d.). Roche Martin. https://www.rochemartin.com/

Perry, E. (2022, June 21). *The 11 communication skills leaders need*. BetterUp. https://www.betterup.com/blog/leadership-communication-skills

Perry, E. (2023, June 20). *Is your team actually working? 10 tips to recognize a good team*. BetterUp. https://www.betterup.com/blog/what-makes-a-good-team

The psychology of employee motivation: Understanding what drives workplace engagement | best NJ insurance. (2023, November 24). Cosmo. https://cosmoins.com/the-psychology-of-employee-motivation-understanding-what-drives-workplace-engagement/

Qualtrics. (2020, May 20). *50 powerful quotes on leadership for your organization*. Qualtrics. https://www.qualtrics.com/blog/50-powerful-leadership-quotes/

Robinson, A. (2018, October 18). *New report says most employees aren't interested in leadership training. here's how to change that*. Inc. https://www.inc.com/adam-robinson/new-report-says-most-employees-arent-interested-in-leadership-training-heres-how-to-change-that.html

Rock, D., & Grant, H. (2016). *Why diverse teams are smarter*. Harvard Business Review. https://hbr.org/2016/11/why-diverse-teams-are-smarter

Sanfilippo, M. (2023, November 20). *How to improve your work-life balance today*. Business News Daily. https://www.businessnewsdaily.com/5244-improve-work-life-balance-today.html

Serban, R. (2017, August 9). *Team dynamics is about playing team roles to your advantage*. Hubgets Blog. https://www.hubgets.com/blog/team-dynamics-belbin-team-roles/

7 tips for communicating with clarity. (n.d.). LinkedIn. https://www.linkedin.com/pulse/20141124154010-7245993-7-tips-for-communicating-with-clarity/

Sherman, F. (2020, July 27). *How do different personalities affect teamwork?* Chron. https://smallbusiness.chron.com/different-personalities-affect-teamwork-11607.html

16 team building case studies and training case studies. (2021, December 21). Outback Team Building & Training. https://www.outbackteambuilding.com/blog/team-building-training-case-studies/

Smit, L. (2016, June 3). *10 communication pitfalls – And how to avoid them*. everywoman. https://www.everywoman.com/my-development/10-communication-pitfalls-and-how-avoid-them/

Square. (2021, October 1). *Time management skills & examples: 7 effective strategies*. The Bottom Line by Square. https://squareup.com/us/en/the-bottom-line/operating-your-business/7-time-management-skills-practiced-by-successful-people

Stanford, C. (2014, July 5). *Adapting communication styles to different audiences*. Fleximize. https://fleximize.com/articles/000592/communication-styles

Steinmann, B., Klug, H. J. P., & Maier, G. W. (2019). The path is the goal: How transformational leaders enhance followers' job attitudes and proactive behavior. *Frontiers in Psychology*, 9(2338). NCBI. https://doi.org/10.3389/fpsyg.2018.02338

A story of leadership growth: Empathy, contextualisation, and appreciation. (2022, June 5). LinkedIn. https://www.linkedin.com/pulse/story-leadership-growth-empathy-contextualisation-appreciation-/

Stumbles, T. (2023, February 28). *How to plan the best team-building activities for work*. Project Management Tips and Tricks. https://www.officetimeline.com/blog/how-to-plan-the-best-team-building-activities-for-work

Team Building. (2018, May 8). *How to plan a successful team building event in 9 easy steps.* Outback Team Building & Training. https://www.outbackteambuilding.com/blog/how-to-plan-a-successful-team-building-event-in-9-easy-steps/

Team building: Learning through the experiential way. (n.d.). Outlife. https://www.outlife.in/-team-building-learning-through-the-experiential-way.html

Team, H. E. (2023, October 13). *Case studies: Impact of emotional intelligence on healthcare leadership success.* Soft Skills for Healthcare. https://esoftskills.com/healthcare/case-studies-impact-of-emotional-intelligence-on-healthcare-leadership-success/

Team, W. (2023, September 25). *The power of transparency in effective leadership.* Wrike. https://www.wrike.com/blog/power-of-transparency/

TeamBuilding. (2022, February 17). *Team building objectives & goals: Basic guide.* Team Building. https://teambuilding.com/blog/team-building-objectives

Ten reasons why diversity in leadership is crucial. (n.d.). Drury University. https://www.drury.edu/business/ten-reasons-why-diversity-in-leadership-is-crucial/

Thornton, P. B. (2021, October 12). *Leadership case studies.* Training. https://trainingmag.com/leadership-case-studies/

Timothy R. Clark psychological safety. (n.d.). Leader Factor. Retrieved January 7, 2024, from https://www.leaderfactor.com/learn/timothy-r-clark-psychological-safety

Tretina, K. (2020, July 31). *Investing basics: How the S&P 500 works.* Forbes Advisor. https://www.forbes.com/advisor/investing/what-is-sp-500/

University of the People. (2020, May 1). *What makes a good team that builds success.* https://www.uopeople.edu/blog/what-makes-a-good-team/

Van Wingerden, J., & Van der Stoep, J. (2018). The motivational potential of meaningful work: Relationships with strengths use, work engagement, and performance. *PLOS ONE, 13*(6), e0197599. https://doi.org/10.1371/journal.pone.0197599

What are some common communication pitfalls and how can you avoid them? (n.d.). LinkedIn. https://www.linkedin.com/advice/0/what-some-common-communication-pitfalls-1e

What are some examples of successful leaders who rely on intuition in decision-making? (n.d.). LinkedIn. https://www.linkedin.com/advice/1/what-some-examples-successful-leaders-who-rely

What are the benefits of adapting your communication style to different audiences? (n.d.). LinkedIn. https://www.linkedin.com/advice/3/what-benefits-adapting-your-communication

IMAGE REFERENCES

Parabol | The Agile Meeting Toolbox. (2021, September 2). *People standing on grey concrete stairs during daytime* [Image]. Unsplash. https://unsplash.com/photos/people-standing-on-gray-concrete-stairs-during-daytime-qSv1gwYEfa8

Distel, A. (2019, May 2). *Man standing in front of group of men* [Image]. Unsplash. https://unsplash.com/s/visual/2ce05f0a-015e-4b34-8f3b-a917abb9e46e

Du Preez, P. (2018, April 9). *Three men laughing while looking in the laptop inside room*

[Image]. Unsplash. https://unsplash.com/photos/three-men-laughing-while-looking-in-the-laptop-inside-room-XkKCui44iM0

geralt. (2017, January 11). *Delegate man businessman hand* [Image]. Pixabay. https://pixabay.com/photos/delegate-man-businessman-hand-1971218/

Goodman, J. (2019a, March 14). *Five person by table watching turned on white iMac* [Image]. Unsplash. https://unsplash.com/photos/five-person-by-table-watching-turned-on-white-imac-vbxyFxlgpjM

Goodman, J. (2019b, March 15). *Woman placing sticky notes on wall* [Image]. Unsplash. https://unsplash.com/s/visual/17b21f02-7df5-47ff-bb39-e51f622356bd

Graham, S. (2016, January 30). *Person holding pencil near laptop computer* [Image]. Unsplash. https://unsplash.com/photos/person-holding-pencil-near-laptop-computer-5fNmWej4tAA

Headway. (2018, February 19). *Man talking in the meeting* [Image]. Unsplash. https://unsplash.com/photos/man-talking-in-the-meeting-jfR5wu2hMI0

Herrmann, S. (2019, February 25). *Four men looking to the paper on table* [Image]. Unsplash. https://unsplash.com/photos/four-men-looking-to-the-paper-on-table-O2o1hzDA7iE

Krukau, Y. (2021, April 25). *People having conflict while working* [Image]. Pexels. https://www.pexels.com/photo/people-having-conflict-while-working-7640830/

Piacquadio, A. (2020, February 17). *Basketball team stacking hands together* [Image]. Pexels. https://www.pexels.com/photo/basketball-team-stacking-hands-together-3755440/

Plavalaguna, D. (2020, December 10). *People cooperating with themselves* [Image]. Pexels. https://www.pexels.com/photo/people-cooperating-with-themselves-6146691/

RDNE Stock project. (2021, April 18). *People sitting on green grass waving their hands* [Image]. Pexels. https://www.pexels.com/photo/people-sitting-on-green-grass-waving-their-hands-7551760/

Samkov, I. (2021, May 29). *Colleagues discussing documents* [Image]. Pexels. https://www.pexels.com/photo/colleagues-discussing-documents-8117472/

SHVETS production. (2021, March 18). *Woman discussing problem during group therapy* [Image]. Pexels. https://www.pexels.com/photo/woman-discussing-problem-during-group-therapy-7176305/

Sikkema, K. (2020, February 9). *Person writing on white paper* [Image]. Unsplash. https://unsplash.com/photos/person-writing-on-white-paper-v9FQR4tbIq8

Startaê Team. (2018, June 16). *Person pointing white paper on wall* [Image]. Unsplash. https://unsplash.com/photos/person-pointing-white-paper-on-wall-7tXA8xwe4W4

StartupStockPhotos. (2015, January 9). *Meeting brainstorming business* [Image]. Pixabay. https://pixabay.com/photos/meeting-brainstorming-business-594091/

Themes, N. (2017, September 1). *Person using black iPad* [Image]. Unsplash. https://unsplash.com/photos/person-using-black-ipad-yyMJNPgQ-X8

Winkler, M. (2023, September 28). *A typewriter with the word resilience building on it* [Image]. Pexels. https://www.pexels.com/photo/a-typewriter-with-the-word-resilience-building-on-it-18536266/

www.ingramcontent.com/pod-product-compliance
Lightning Source LLC
Chambersburg PA
CBHW070710130626
46553CB00005B/1931